Michael M. Dediu

All People ask for Peace + Freedom =
Prosperity

Moving from local conflicts to world peace and freedom

DERC Publishing House

Nashua, New Hampshire, U. S. A.

Published and printed in the
United States of America
On the Great Seal of the United States are included:
E Pluribus Unum (Out of many, one)
Annuit Coeptis (He has approved of the undertakings)
Novus Ordo Seclorum (New order of the ages)

Library of Congress Control Number: 2021903110

Dediu, Michael M.

All people ask for Peace + Freedom = Prosperity
Moving from local conflicts to world peace and freedom

ISBN-13: 978-1-950999-31-6

MSG0574654_uJ7GR4t8y0qk8ees0fBy
1-10184885321
1-4OFVJIB
08685D
26RA607V
1-4OFVJII

Preface

For many thousands of years people are looking for the right formula for a good life – this book provides this formula for all people on the Peaceful Terra:

Peace + Freedom + Good Health + Good Family + Good Education + Good Jobs + Harmony = Prosperity + Happiness

Socrates: "The secret of change is to focus all your energy, not on fighting the old, but on building the new" – exactly this we are doing in this book, giving many details about how to change in better, for the benefit of all people, from working together to establish a permanent peace, freedom and prosperity on our planet, to expanding the space exploration, which will help future generations to move to other planets, asteroids, etc.

There are many **g**lobal challenges – they can be solved if all people have peace, freedom, good health, good education, good jobs, good science & technology, harmony and prosperity for all.

William Shakespeare – "One touch of nature makes the whole world kin."

Our Peaceful Terra is so beautiful – let's make it also very friendly, harmonious and full of freedom and happiness!

Michael M. Dediu, Ph. D.

Nashua, New Hampshire, U. S. A., 18 February 2021

On 7th Avenue at West 57th Street, looking southwest: right: a classical building, which is tangent to the right, on W 57th St, to the American Fine Arts Society building (1892); left down: a beautiful building, opposite Carnegie Hall (to the left, across 7th Ave, 1891, concert hall with exceptional acoustics, architecture and performance history); left up: an impressive double skyscraper, with the southwest side on W 56th St.

Table of Contents

France, Paris: The upper part of the western façade of Cathédrale
Notre Dame de Paris (1163 – 1345, 90 m), on the south-eastern part
of the Île de la Cité, which is considered the center of Paris, in the
fourth arrondissement. The organ has 7,374 pipes, with about 900
classified as historical. It has 110 real stops, five 56-key manuals
and a 32-key pedalboard; it is now fully computerized. The Towers
at Notre-Dame contain five church bells. The great bourdon bell,
Emmanuel, from 1681, 13 t, is located in the South Tower (right).

Formula issue 1. Elimination of war

Description: This issue (for the Peace element of the formula) is simply to work for the elimination of war and any type of conflicts on Earth, making possible for all the people on Earth to live better, peacefully, free, healthy, and prosperous.

Formula solution: Using computers and the Internet, general instructions will be given to all.

Starting day: 1 May 2021

Ending day: continuous

Salary: From the minimum wage to over $100,000/year

Possibility of improving the solution or give another idea: Yes, for good performers.

Comments: It is a matter of common sense – all people want peace, freedom, good health, harmony and prosperity.
For all these issues, people will work in well-organized institutions, with a very clear and urgent objectives.

Self-managing initiatives are always welcome: self-managing is the highest form of work, and will be achieved at beginning by the most talented people, but then more and more people will join them.

Self-management includes: establishing goals, timeline and deadlines, meeting deadlines, planning to complete projects, organizing information and materials, being trustworthy, extending trust to employees, recognizing mistakes and your limitations, transforming yourself, being a servant leader, setting the overall direction of a task, and employees implementing the details with minimal oversight.

Full trust in people will be achieved after implementing the Constitution of the World.

No war + Peace + Freedom + Good Health + Good Family + Good Education + Good Jobs + Harmony = Prosperity + Happiness

Italy, Rome: The Amphitheatrum Flavium (Colosseum, 80 AD, left), the Arch of Constantine (315 AD, right), and a carabiniere wedding photo event.

USA, Boston: a view of the north-east part of Boston, from Cambridge, over Charles River Basin. Federal Reserve Bank Building (187 m, left), and other tall buildings in the financial district.

Formula issue 2. Establishing a permanent peace

Description: The objective of this issue is to have a lasting peace, without any conflicts on Earth, making possible for all the people on Earth to live better, peacefully, free, healthy, and prosperous.

Formula solution: Using computers and the Internet, general instructions will be given to all.

Starting day: 1 May 2021

Ending day: continuous

Salary: From $20,000/year.

Possibility of improving the solution or give another idea: Yes, for good performers.

Comments: It is a matter of common sense – living on the same planet, all people want peace, freedom, good health, harmony and prosperity.

It is not sufficient to just eliminate war - we need to build a very strong and long-lasting Peace, because without peace not much else can be done. People want a Peaceful Terra.

Having a lasting peace, without any conflicts on Earth, is relatively easy, if dedicated people keep working on it, using self-management.

Permanent Peace + Freedom + Good Health + Good Family + Good Education + Good Jobs + Harmony = Prosperity + Happiness

Formula issue 3. Taking care of 509 M km² of land and water

Description: The objective of this issue is to properly manage all the planet for all people.

Formula solution: Using computers and the Internet, general instructions will be given to all, by people with knowledge and experience in this area.

Starting day: 1 May 2021

Ending day: continuous work.

Salary: From $20,000year.

Possibility of improving the solution or give another idea: Yes.

Comments: The people will always have priority, with a proper balance. People will work for self-supporting institutions, which focus on clean and beautiful Earth for all people.

Land and water always created conflicts – now, finally, all people will enjoy all the land and water, for their benefit, without any conflicts.

Water purification and recycling is an essential world project.

All land and water management + Peace + Freedom + Good Health + Good Family + Good Education + Good Jobs + Harmony = Prosperity + Happiness

Formula issue 4. Less bureaucratic rules

Description: The objective of this issue is simply to eliminate the many superfluous rules, which create bureaucracy.

Formula solution: Using computers and the Internet, general instructions will be given to all by people with knowledge and experience in this area.

Starting day: 1 May 2021

Ending day: continuous

Salary: From $20,000/year

Possibility of improving the solution or give another idea: Yes.

Comments: This will be a continuous effort by all people - those who get excellent results will be compensated. It is clear – no need of bureaucracy on the planet!

No bureaucracy + Peace + Freedom + Good Health + Good Family + Good Education + Good Jobs + Harmony = Prosperity + Happiness

Italy, Rome: The south-west side of the Amphitheatrum Flavium (or Colosseum, 80 AD), with a flag throwing festival on December 8, 2011.

Formula issue 5. Create 10 friendly regions

Description: The objective of this issue is to create the conditions for a good and efficient management of the country Peaceful Terra.

Formula solution: Using computers and the Internet, general instructions will be given to all by people with knowledge and experience in this area.

Starting day: 1 May 2021

Ending day: 6 months after the starting day.

Salary: From $48,000

Possibility of improving the solution or give another idea: Yes.

Comments: All people will participate. For easier administration, Peaceful Terra will be only administratively divided in 10 simple and friendly regions of around 770 M people each, called R0, R1,…, R9, which will be delimited by meridians (or line of longitudes), with the assistance of the United Nations.

A huge country needs administrative division.

10 friendly regions + Peace + Freedom + Good Health + Good Family + Good Education + Good Jobs + Harmony = Prosperity + Happiness

Formula issue 6. Transform cities in capitals

Description: The objective of this issue is to begin work for the preparation of many cities, which will become capitals.

Formula solution: People with knowledge and experience in this area will design a plan for self-managing this task, when possible.

Starting day: 1 May 2021

Ending day: 6 months after the starting day.

Salary: From $32,000/year

Possibility of improving the solution or give another idea: Yes.

Comments: Capitals will be everywhere, because the current capitals tend to become huge bureaucracies, with lots of people trying to be there, without much usefulness. Peaceful Terra will have moving capitals, to benefit everybody.

Each region will have a pair of capitals plus an outside city, for better and more homogenous management. (all will change every year; more details are in the book "World with One Country & its Ten Friendly Regions - Moving from 195 disagreeing countries, to 1 country with 10 collaborating regions"). For example, the first implementation will be:

R0 between meridians 0 and 15^0 E, capitals: Bern (Switzerland), Libreville (Gabon), and Oxford (UK).

R1: 15^0 E - 30^0 E, Warsaw (Poland), Pretoria (South Africa) and Miami (FL, USA).

R2: 30^0 E - 45^0 E, Moscow (Russia), Cairo (Egypt), and Grenoble (France).

R3: 45^0 E - 75^0 E, Astana (Kazakhstan), Karachi (Pakistan), and Montpellier (France).

R4: 75^0 E - 85^0 E, New Delhi (India), Novosibirsk (Russia), and Magdeburg (Germany).

R5: 85^0 E - 100^0 E, Krasnoyarsk (Russia), Urumqi (China), and Avignon (France).

R6: 100^0 E - 115^0 E, Jakarta (Indonesia), Beijing (China), and Neuchâtel (Switzerland).

R7: 115^0 E - 180^0, Tokyo (Japan), Sydney (Australia), and Malmö (Sweden).

R8: 180^0 - 70^0 Washington (USA), Mexico City (Mexico), and Bellinzona (Switzerland).

R9: 70^0 W – 0 Halifax (Canada), Brasilia (Brazil), and Biel (Switzerland).

There are many big differences between the number of people in different regions, in the first implementation, and then between the populations of different sub-regions, but this is just the first implementation, which needs to be quickly put in place, and then, very easily, the delimitations will be moved a few kilometers east or west, to reach a balanced population (same number of people).

Because all the people are in the same country, it is normal to modify a little its regions, for better administration, to make everybody happy.

It is well understood that there will be some difficulties in the beginning, like in all beginnings, but with calm, patience, perseverance and hard work, the things will improve fast, and all the people will enjoy a better life.

New capitals + Peace + Freedom + Good Health + Good Family + Good Education + Good Jobs + Harmony = Prosperity + Happiness

Japan, Hiroshima: 17 April 2015, Bell of Peace (1964), The Greek inscription on the bell is Socrates' aphorism "Know yourself".

Formula issue 7. Work on sub-regions and districts

Description: The objective of this issue is to define the sub-regions and districts, for better administration of the help for people.

Formula solution: People with knowledge and experience in this area will design a plan for self-managing this task.

Starting day: 1 July 2021

Ending day: 6 months after the starting day.

Salary: From $29,000/year

Possibility of improving the solution or give another idea: Yes.

Comments: Each of the 10 regions will be divided by meridians in 10 sub-regions S00, , S99, each with about 77 M people.

Then each of the 100 sub-regions will be divided in 10 districts: D000, D001, , D999, each with about 7.7 M people, and each of the districts will have their current small and big cities.

All these delimitations between regions, as well as between sub-regions, will be flexible: these will be just simple administrative delimitations – they will be changed after each census (5 years), for maintaining a balanced number of people in all regions (around 770 M) and sub-regions (around 77 M).

New sub-regions and districts + Peace + Freedom + Good Health + Good Family + Good Education + Good Jobs + Harmony = Prosperity + Happiness

Formula issue 8. Help to have telework for all

Description: The objective of this issue is to extend and improve telework for all.

Formula solution: People with knowledge and experience in this area will design a plan for self-managing this task.

Starting day: 1 May 2021

Ending day: continuous

Salary: From $28,000/year

Possibility of improving the solution or give another idea: Yes.

Comments: This is the future – with telework many people will have a northern residence and a southern residence, seasonally moving from one to the other, to avoid extreme cold or heat, and having the same hour.

Telework + Peace + Freedom + Good Health + Good Family + Good Education + Good Jobs + Harmony = Prosperity + Happiness

Formula issue 9. Enjoyable oceans for all

Description: The objective of this issue is to carefully manage all the oceans for all the people.

Formula solution: People with knowledge and experience in this area will design a plan for self-managing this task.

Starting day: 1 May 2021

Ending day: continuous

Salary: From $35,000/year

Possibility of improving the solution or give another idea: Yes.

Comments: The oceans are important for people and for our planet. All the oceans will belong to some of the regions, therefore will be maintained by those regions, to be free of any piracy or other bad activity – World Police will help when necessary.

Enjoyable oceans + Peace + Freedom + Good Health + Good Family + Good Education + Good Jobs + Harmony = Prosperity + Happiness

Germany - 23 March 1978, Freibourg im Breisgau (1120 by Duke Berthold III of Zähringen (1085-1122), elevation 278 m, the south façade of Freiburger Münster (cathedral, 1200, 116 m, J. S. Bach (1685-1750) performed here).

.

Formula issue 10. Explain the World Government

Description: The objective of this issue is to keep people correctly informed about the World Government, in order to improve it.

Formula solution: People with knowledge and experience in this area will design a plan for self-managing this task.

Starting day: 1 May 2021

Ending day: continuous

Salary: From $25,000/year

Possibility of improving the solution or give another idea: Yes.

Comments: It is important for people to know the World Government, in order to have peace, freedom, good health, harmony and prosperity. Peaceful Terra, with its family of over 7.7 B people, will have four levels of world management: at the local level, if needed, it could be one or two more levels of local managers (mayors, town managers, county managers – all levels of management must be friendly, helpful, fast, polite, modest and smart):

Level 1 Managers: 1,000 L1 friendly managers, for the 1,000 districts, who will supervise and assist the mayors and town managers from their district, for a total of about 7,700,000 people in each district. Each of the 1,000 L1 friendly managers will be located in a central city from their districts – they could be the mayors of those cities, but with new responsibilities for the whole district.

Level 2 Formula solution: 100 L2 friendly managers, for the 100 sub-regions, who will supervise and assist the 10 L1 managers of the 10 districts of each sub-region, for a total of about 77,000,000 people for each sub-region. These 100 L2 friendly managers will move each month between the two capitals of each of the 100 sub-regions.

Level 3 Managers: 10 L3 friendly managers for the 10 regions.

Level 4 Managers: 10 L4 friendly advisers for the world.

Good World Government + Peace + Freedom + Good Health + Good Family + Good Education + Good Jobs + Harmony = Prosperity + Happiness

Paris: Rue Soufflot (from Panthéon, looking north-west to Jardin du Luxembourg (1612, back), and Tour Eiffel (1889, 324 m)), with the Université Paris 1 Panthéon-Sorbonne (1150, 1971, right).

Formula issue 11. Work on the two capitals for each sub-region

Description: The objective of this issue is to prepare 200 cities to be sub-region capitals.

Formula solution: People with knowledge and experience in this area will create a self-managing plan.

Starting day: 1 May 2021

Ending day: 6 months after the starting day

Salary: From 36,000/year

Possibility of improving the solution or give another idea: Yes.

Comments: It is relevant to have many cities refreshed and prepared to be capitals of sub-regions.
        For example: in the beginning these capitals will be:

In Region R0: from Paris (France) to N'Djamena (Chad)

- The sub-region R00 will have the capitals Paris (France) and Niamey (Niger) – assistance from Magdeburg (Germany).
- The sub-region R01 will have the capitals Brussels (Belgium) and Porto-Novo (Benin) - assistance from Toronto (Canada).
- The sub-region R02 will have the capitals Amsterdam (Netherlands) and Algiers (Algeria) - assistance from Graz (Austria).
- The sub-region R03 will have the capitals Luxembourg (Luxembourg) and Sao Tome (Sao Tome and Principe) - assistance from Adelaide (Australia).
- The sub-region R04 will have the capitals of Abuja (Nigeria) and Bochum (Germany) - assistance from Nikko (Japan).

- The sub-region R05 will have the capitals Malabo (Equatorial Guinea), and Zürich (Switzerland) - assistance from Leeds (UK).
- The sub-region R06 will have the capitals Oslo (Norway) and Tunis (Tunisia) - assistance from Sheffield (UK).
- The sub-region R07 will have the capitals Roma (Italy) and Luanda (Angola) - assistance from Yamagata (Japan).
- The sub-region R08 will have the capitals in Berlin (Germany) and Tripoli (Libya) - assistance from New York (USA).
- The sub-region R09 will have the capitals Prague (Czech Republic) and N'Djamena (Chad) - assistance from Brisbane (Australia).

France, Paris: The south-west façade of Palais de Chaillot (1937, left) and the north-west side of Tour Eiffel (1889, 324 m), from Place du Trocadéro et du 11 Novembre.

Switzerland: Lausanne (Roman 150, 147,000, 41 km^2, 500 m elevation), marina on Lac Léman, southwest of Place de la Navigation (right).

In Region R1: from Zagreb (Croatia) to Bujumbura (Burundi)

- The sub-region R10 will have the capitals in Zagreb (Croatia) and Brazzaville (Congo) - assistance from Nantes (France).
- The sub-region R11 will have the capitals in Vienna (Austria), Windhoek (Namibia) - assistance from Bilbao (Spain).
- The sub-region R12 will have the capitals in Stockholm (Sweden), Bangui (Central African Republic) - assistance from Florence (Italy).
- The sub-region R13 will have the capitals in Budapest (Hungary), Rundu (Namibia) - assistance from Monaco (Monaco).
- The sub-region R14 will have the capitals in Belgrade (Serbia), Kananga (Democratic Republic of Congo) - assistance from Liverpool (UK).
- The sub-region R15 will have the capitals in Athens (Greece), Mongu (Zambia) - assistance from Los Angeles (CA, USA).
- The sub-region R16 will have the capitals in Helsinki (Finland) and Kolwezi (Democratic Republic of the Congo) - assistance from Montreal (Canada).
- The sub-region R17 will have the capitals in Bucharest (Romania) and Gaborone (Botswana) - assistance from Philadelphia (PA, USA).
- The sub-region R18 will have the capitals in Minsk (Belarus) and Maseru (Lesotho) - assistance from Orleans (France).
- The sub-region R19 will have the capitals in Chisinau (Republic of Moldova) and Bujumbura (Burundi) - assistance from Hamburg (Germany).

France: Le Lac du Bourget, the southernmost end of the Jura Mountains, the department of Savoie, elevation 232 m, 45 km^2, 18 km by 3.5 km.

Chicago (Illinois, 1833, 2.7 million): Belmont Harbor (6 km north from downtown) on Lake Michigan (58,000 km^2, 494 km by 190 km, 176 m surface elevation, depth 281 m (max), 85 m (average)).

In Region R2: from Kiev (Ukraine) to Baghdad (Iraq)

- The sub-region R20 will have the capitals in Kiev (Ukraine) and Kigali (Rwanda) - assistance from Ottawa (Canada).
- The sub-region R21 will have the capitals in Ankara (Turkey) and Khartoum (Sudan) - assistance from Salzburg (Austria).
- The sub-region R22 will have the capitals in Lilongwe (Malawi) and Nicosia (Cyprus) - assistance from Dallas (TX, USA).
- The sub-region R23 will have the capitals in Jerusalem (Israel) and Dodoma (Tanzania) - assistance from Strasbourg (France).
- The sub-region R24 will have the capitals in Damascus (Syria) and Nairobi (Kenya) - assistance from Stuttgart (Germany).
- The sub-region R25 will have the capitals in Krasnodar (Russia) and Addis Ababa (Ethiopia) - assistance from Marseille (France).
- The sub-region R26 will have the capitals in Rostov-on-Don (Russia) and Asmara (Eritrea) - assistance from Leipzig (Germany).
- The sub-region R27 will have the capitals in Stavropol (Russia) and Djibouti (Djibouti) - assistance from Zürich (Switzerland).
- The sub-region R28 will have the capitals in Mosul (Iraq) and Moroni (Comoros) - assistance from Linz (Austria).
- The sub-region R29 will have the capitals in Yerevan (Armenia) and Baghdad (Iraq) - assistance from Göttingen (Germany).

Japan: on route 137, on the south-east side of Lake Kawaguchi (6 km², 830 m elevation, 100 km south-west of Tokyo, 17 km north of Mt Fuji (3,776 m)), the bridge for route 707, the city Oishi (center-left), and Mount. Kurodake (back).

In Region R3: from Riyadh (Saudi Arabia) to Malé (Maldives)

- The sub-region R30 will have the capitals in Riyadh (Saudi Arabia) and Mogadishu (Somalia) - assistance from Bonn (Germany).
- The sub-region R31 will have the capitals in Baku (Azerbaijan) and Antananarivo (Madagascar) - assistance from Le Mans (France).
- The sub-region R32 will have the capitals in Oral (Kazakhstan) and Tehran (Iran) - assistance from Pisa (Italy).
- The sub-region R33 will have the capitals in Ashgabat (Turkmenistan) and Abu Dhabi (United Arab Emirates) - assistance from Wolfsburg (Germany).
- The sub-region R34 will have the capitals in Magnitogorsk (Russia) and Muscat (Oman) - assistance from Toulouse (France).
- The sub-region R35 will have the capitals in Chelyabinsk (Russia) and Herat (Afghanistan) - assistance from Basel (Switzerland).
- The sub-region R36 will have the capitals in Tyumen (Russia) and Kandahar (Afghanistan) - assistance from Nagoya (Japan).
- The sub-region R37 will have the capitals in Dushanbe (Tajikistan) and Labytnangi (Russia) - assistance from Limoges (France).
- The sub-region R38 will have the capitals in Tashkent (Uzbekistan) and Kabul (Afghanistan) - assistance from Rostock (Germany).
- The sub-region R39 will have the capitals in Islamabad (Pakistan) and Malé (Maldives) - assistance from La Rochelle (France).

Switzerland: Geneva (121 BC), from the pier, buildings on Quai Gustave Ador near Rue Muzy, marina on Lac Léman (372 m elevation, 580 km^2),

In Region R4: from Bishkek (Kyrgyzstan) to Brahmapur (India)

- The sub-region R40 will have the capitals in Bishkek (Kyrgyzstan) and Jaipur (India) - assistance from Osaka (Japan).
- The sub-region R41 will have the capitals in Akola (India) and Kashgar (China) - assistance from Genoa (Italy).
- The sub-region R42 will have the capitals in Almaty (Kazakhstan) and Coimbatore (India) - assistance from Perth (Australia).
- The sub-region R43 will have the capitals in Kuybyshev (Russia) and Agra (India) - assistance from Fukuoka (Japan).
- The sub-region R44 will have the capitals in Vertikos (Russia) and Nagpur (India) - assistance from Coral Bay (Australia).
- The sub-region R45 will have the capitals in Chennai (India) and Colombo (Sri Lanka) - assistance from Sapporo (Japan).
- The sub-region R46 will have the capitals in Lucknow (India) and Fedosikha (Russia) - assistance from Niigata (Japan).
- The sub-region R47 will have the capitals in Bilaspur (India) and Kolpashevo (Russia) - assistance from Albany (Australia).
- The sub-region R48 will have the capitals in Visakhapatnam (India) and Barnaul (Russia) - assistance from Hiroshima (Japan).
- The sub-region R49 will have the capitals in Brahmapur (India) and Tomsk (Russia) - assistance from Yokohama (Japan).

Switzerland: Lausanne (Roman 150, 147,000, 41 km², 500 m elevation, 62 km northeast of Geneva, the home of the International Olympic Committee), marina on Lac Léman, southwest of Place de la Navigation (right).

In Region R5: from Kathmandu (Nepal) to Dehong (China)

- The sub-region R50 will have the capitals in Kathmandu (Nepal) and Patna (India) - assistance from Kobe (Japan).
- The sub-region R51 will have the capitals in Bayingol (China) and Novokuznetsk (Russia) - assistance from Vichy (France).
- The sub-region R52 will have the capitals in Thimphu (Bhutan) and Dhaka (Bangladesh) - assistance from Jena (Germany).
- The sub-region R53 will have the capitals in Lhasa (China) and Achinsk (Russia) - assistance from Reims (France).
- The sub-region R54 will have the capitals in Abakan (Russia) and Kumul (China) - assistance from Fribourg (Switzerland).
- The sub-region R55 will have the capitals in Kyzyl (Russia) and Dibrugarh (India) - assistance from Denmark (Australia).
- The sub-region R56 will have the capitals in Bassein (Myanmar) and Tinsukia (India) - assistance from Chiba (Japan).
- The sub-region R57 will have the capitals in Yushu City (China) and Tinskoy (Russia) - assistance from Klagenfurt (Austria).
- The sub-region R58 will have the capitals in Jiuquan (China) and Medan (Indonesia) - assistance from Lucerne (Switzerland).
- The sub-region R59 will have the capitals in Chiang Mai (Thailand) and Dehong (China) - assistance from Mulhouse (France).

USA, Gloucester: At the northeast end of the Gloucester Harbor (Inner Harbor, right up), looking east to the dry dock for repairs of the ships Privateer IV 7 Seas Whale Watch & Charters (left), and Massachusetts (right).

In Region R6: from Bangkok (Thailand) to Chita (Russia)

- The sub-region R60 will have the capitals in Bangkok (Thailand) and Kuala Lumpur (Malaysia) - assistance from Besançon (France).
- The sub-region R61 will have the capitals in Vientiane (Laos) and Singapore – assistance from Freiburg im Breisgau (Germany).
- The sub-region R62 will have the capitals in Phnom Penh (Cambodia) and Irkutsk (Russia) – assistance from Baden (Switzerland).
- The sub-region R63 will have the capitals in Palembang (Indonesia), Hanoi (Vietnam) – assistance from Thun (Switzerland).
- The sub-region R64 will have the capitals in Ulan Bator (Mongolia) and Ulan-Ude (Russia) – assistance from Chaumont (France).
- The sub-region R65 will have the capitals in Cirebon (Indonesia) and Nanning (China) – assistance from Vaduz (Lichtenstein).
- The sub-region R66 will have the capitals in Pontianak (Indonesia) and Baotou (China) – assistance from Lugano (Switzerland).
- The sub-region R67 will have the capitals in Surakarta (Indonesia) and Yichang (China) – assistance from Thonon-les-Bain (France).
- The sub-region R68 will have the capitals in Surabaya (Indonesia) and Changsha (China) – assistance from Burgdorf (Switzerland).
- The sub-region R69 will have the capitals in Chita (Russia) and Hong Kong (China) – assistance from Colmar (France).

USA, New York: On W 32nd St, looking east, before Ave of the Americas and Broadway: Empire State Building (center back) Manhattan Mall (left), Radisson Martinique on Broadway Hotel (center down).

In Region R7: from Nanchang (China) to Melbourne (Australia)

- The sub-region R70 will have the capitals in Bandar Seri Begawan (Brunei Darussalam) and Nanchang (China) – assistance from Turku (Finland).
- The sub-region R71 will have the capitals in Krasnokamensk (Russia) and Jinan (China) – assistance from St. Gallen (Switzerland).
- The sub-region R72 will have the capitals in Baguio City (Philippines) and Hangzhou (China) – assistance from Dole (France).
- The sub-region R73 will have the capitals in Manila (Philippines) and Taipei (Taiwan, China) – assistance from Metz (France).
- The sub-region R74 will have the capitals in Kupang (Indonesia) and Shanghai (China) – assistance from Davos (Switzerland).
- The sub-region R75 will have the capitals in Pyongyang (North Korea) and Seoul (South Korea) – assistance from Versailles (France).
- The sub-region R76 will have the capitals in Vladivostok (Russia) and Busan (South Korea) – assistance from Innsbruck (Austria).
- The sub-region R77 will have the capitals in Kyoto (Japan) and Khabarovsk (Russia) – assistance from Germering (Germany).
- The sub-region R78 will have the capitals in Nagoya (Japan) and Komsomolsk-on-Amur (Russia) – assistance from Venice (Italy).
- The sub-region R79 will have the capitals in Sendai (Japan) and Melbourne (Australia) – assistance from St. Moritz (Switzerland).

Italy, Venezia: Gondole and water taxi with Danieli Excelsior (back), the second building after Palazzo Ducale on Riva degli Schiavoni.

In Region R8: from Anchorage (Alaska, USA) to Lima (Peru)

- The sub-region R80 will have the capitals in Uelen (Russia) and Anchorage (Alaska, USA), – assistance from Zug (Switzerland).
- The sub-region R81 will have the capitals in Vancouver (Canada) and San Jose (CA, USA) – assistance from Odense (Denmark).
- The sub-region R82 will have the capitals in Vernon (Canada) and Los Angeles (CA, USA) – assistance from Amstetten (Austria).
- The sub-region R83 will have the capitals in Calgary (Canada) and Tijuana (Mexico) – assistance from Chur (Switzerland).
- The sub-region R84 will have the capitals in Hermosillo (Mexico) and Tucson (AR, USA) – assistance from Bergen (Norway).
- The sub-region R85 will have the capitals in Chihuahua (Mexico) and Regina (Canada) – assistance from Gothenburg (Sweden).
- The sub-region R86 will have the capitals in San Luis Potosi City (Mexico) and Winnipeg (Canada) – assistance from Yverdon-les-Bains (Switzerland).
- The sub-region R87 will have the capitals in Tulsa (OK, USA) and Veracruz (Mexico) – assistance from Bregenz (Austria).
- The sub-region R88 will have the capitals in Memphis (TN, USA) and San José (Costa Rica) – assistance from Uppsala (Sweden).
- The sub-region R89 will have the capitals in Lima (Peru) and Boston (MA, USA) – assistance from Tampere (Finland).

USA, Boston (1630), near the Fish Pier, a tall ship

In Region R9: from La Paz (Bolivia) to London (United Kingdom)

- The sub-region R90 will have the capitals in La Paz (Bolivia) and Bangor (Maine, USA) – assistance from Aosta (Italy).
- The sub-region R91 will have the capitals in Caracas (Venezuela) and Road Town (British Virgin Islands) – assistance from Obergoms (Switzerland).
- The sub-region R92 will have the capitals in Buenos Aires (Argentina) and Fort-de-France (Martinique) – assistance from Freudenstadt (Germany).
- The sub-region R93 will have the capitals in Asuncion (Paraguay) and Montevideo (Uruguay) – assistance from Winterthur (Switzerland).
- The sub-region R94 will have the capitals in Cayenne (French Guiana), St. John's (Canada) – assistance from Novara (Italy).
- The sub-region R95 will have the capitals in Rio de Janeiro (Brazil) and Dakar (Senegal) – assistance from Toyama (Japan).
- The sub-region R96 will have the capitals in Freetown (Sierra Leone) and Lisbon (Portugal) – assistance from Kawasaki (Japan).
- The sub-region R97 will have the capitals in Bamako (Mali) and Athlone (Ireland) – assistance from Ulm (Germany).
- The sub-region R98 will have the capitals in Yamoussoukro (Cote d'Ivoire) and Madrid (Spain) – assistance from Okayama (Japan).
- The sub-region R99 will have the capitals in Ouagadougou (Burkina Faso) and London (United Kingdom) - assistance from Vaasa (Finland).

Two capitals for each region + Peace + Freedom + Good Health + Good Family + Good Education + Good Jobs + Harmony = Prosperity + Happiness

UK, Cambridge, a bas-relief on the eastern wall of the western building of the Old Court (1451) of Queens' College (1448), University of Cambridge, 60 m east of the Mathematical Bridge (1749).

Formula issue 12. Explain the Level 3 Management

Description: The objective of this issue is to make people familiar with this Level 3 Management.

Formula solution: People with knowledge and experience in this area will give some general guidelines for self-management.

Starting day: 1 May 2021

Ending day: 4 months after starting

Salary: From $34,000/year

Possibility of improving the solution or give another idea: Yes.

Comments: It is useful to have informed people. The ten L3 friendly managers for the 10 regions will supervise and assist the 10 L2 managers of the 10 sub-regions of each region, for a total of about 770,000,000 people for each region.
   For example, the Region R0 will have the first capitals in

Bern (Switzerland) and Libreville (Gabon) – assistance from Oxford (UK).

For better quality and consistency of the Formula solution, we'll have the first two cities from the region R0, and the third city from outside. Actually, being inside the same country Terra, any city, sub-region or region can ask for advice or help from anybody.

- The Region R1 will have the first capitals in

Warsaw (Poland) and Pretoria (South Africa) – assistance from Miami (FL, USA).

- The Region R2 will have the first capitals in

Moscow (Russia) and Cairo (Egypt) – assistance from Grenoble (France).

- The Region R3 will have the first capitals in

Astana (Kazakhstan) and Karachi (Pakistan), – assistance from Montpellier (France).

Italy, Venezia: The central part of the east façade of Sansovino's Libreria (1537 – 1591) with Biblioteca Marciana (with Tiziano's and Tintoretto's paintings).

- The Region R4 will have the first capitals in

New Delhi (India) and Novosibirsk (Russia) – assistance from Magdeburg (Germany).

- The Region R5 will have the first capitals in

Krasnoyarsk (Russia) and Urumqi (China) – assistance from Avignon (France).

- The Region R6 will have the first capitals in

Jakarta (Indonesia) and Beijing (China) – assistance from Neuchâtel (Switzerland).

- The Region R7 will have the first capitals in

Tokyo (Japan) and Sydney (Australia) – assistance from Malmö (Sweden).

- The Region R8 will have the first capitals in

Washington (USA) and Mexico City (Mexico) – assistance from Bellinzona (Switzerland).

- The Region R9 will have the first capitals in

Halifax (Canada) and Brasilia (Brazil) – assistance from Biel (Switzerland).

Managing the world from these 30 cities + Peace + Freedom + Good Health + Good Family + Good Education + Good Jobs + Harmony = Prosperity + Happiness

Formula issue 13. Explain the Level 4 Management

Description: The objective of this issue is to make people familiar with this Level 4 Management.

Formula solution: People with knowledge and experience in this area will prepare a simple plan for self-management.

Starting day: 1 May 2021

Ending day: 4 months after starting

Salary: From $35,000/year

Possibility of improving the solution or give another idea: Yes.

Comments: It is really important to know well to top Management. The level 4 Management are the very friendly 10 Advisers of the world which will supervise and assist the 10 L3 managers of the 10 regions of the Earth, for a total of about 7,700,000,000 people – all the people on Earth, citizens of Peaceful Terra.

Friendly top management + Peace + Freedom + Good Health + Good Family + Good Education + Good Jobs + Harmony = Prosperity + Happiness

Formula issue 14. Work on locations for the 10 Advisors

Description: The objective of this issue is to transform many cities by having advisors located there.

Formula solution: People with knowledge and experience in this area will prepare a self-management plan.

Starting day: 1 May 2021

Ending day: continuous

Salary: From $34,000/year

Possibility of improving the solution or give another idea: Yes.

Comments: It is an easy and simple Global Task, but important. The 10 Advisors will be located each in one the ten Regions R0, R1,…, R9. For example, in the beginning, for the first month (then changing every month), the ten Advisers of the world will be located:

- in R0: Barcelona (Spain)
- in R1: Benghazi (Libya)
- in R2: Addis Ababa (Ethiopia)
- in R3: Hyderabad (Pakistan)
- in R4: Bhopal (India)
- in R5: Mandalay (Myanmar)
- in R6: Nanchong (China)
- in R7: Khabarovsk (Russia)
- in R8: Houston (USA)
- in R9: Recife (Brazil)

These ten L4 Advisers will be in permanent contact with each other, and with the L3 Advisers, for the best Management of the world.

The ten L4 Advisers will move each month from a first capital of a region to the second capital of another region, at random (or based on urgency, if an emergency occurred). This mobility is essential for having a long period of tranquility and harmony.

The Advisors will be located in the current government buildings, and the excess government buildings and properties will be sold, in order to increase the budget, and to reduce the expenses.

Friendly Advisers in these 10 cities + Peace + Freedom + Good Health + Good Family + Good Education + Good Jobs + Harmony = Prosperity + Happiness

Switzerland, Geneva, on Pont du Mont Blanc (1862, 1965, 252 m X 26.8 m, over Rhône river), going northwest, Les Bergues Hotel (1834) (center

Formula issue 15. Maintain technical equipment for the 10 Advisors

Description: The objective of this issue is to have good equipment for the top 10 Advisers (and all the others), who will collaborate via e-mail, telephone, videoconferences, mail, or face to face, when needed, to produce practical results for all people, very fast.

Formula solution: People with knowledge and experience in this area will prepare a self-management plan.

Starting day: 1 May 2021

Ending day: continuous

Salary: From $36,000/year

Possibility of improving the solution or give another idea: Yes.

Comments: It is essential to have advanced systems for the top Management. The ten L4 Advisers will work by consensus only. It is expected that the 10 Advisors are talented enough to be able to negotiate fast any disagreements between them, and quickly arrive at the best common decision, for the benefit of all people.

Harmonious and constructive top management + Peace + Freedom + Good Health + Good Family + Good Education + Good Jobs + Harmony = Prosperity + Happiness

Formula issue 16. Working on elections for the 10 Advisors

Description: The objective of this issue is to have quiet and civilized elections for the top Managers.

Formula solution: People with knowledge and experience in this area will prepare a self-management plan.

Starting day: 1 May 2021

Ending day: continuous

Salary: From $35,000/year

Possibility of improving the solution or give another idea: Yes.

Comments: It is a high priority to have good, calm and friendly elections.

The ten L4 Advisers will be elected from the 10 regions, and each of them will be the First Adviser (***First among equals*** – from Latin: Primus inter pares) for one month, by rotation.

The First Adviser only coordinates the work of the other 9 Advisors for one month.

Good, calm and friendly elections + Peace + Freedom + Good Health + Good Family + Good Education + Good Jobs + Harmony = Prosperity + Happiness

Formula issue 17. Handle reports from the 10 Advisors

Description: The objective of this issue is to keep people informed about the activities of the top 10 Advisors.

Formula solution: People with knowledge and experience in this area will prepare a self-management plan.

Starting day: 1 June 2021

Ending day: continuous

Salary: From $37,600/year

Possibility of improving the solution or give another idea: Yes.

Comments: It is imperative to correctly inform people by using a Monthly World Report.

    The First Adviser, on the last day of each month, will present in writing for the world (no more than 5 standard pages) a clear and precise Monthly World Report, with a list of finished and unfinished tasks.

    The other 9 Advisers will add their comments to the Monthly World Report (no more than half a page each - total report less than 9.5 pages).

    In order to better know the world government, to help it, and, especially, to improve it, all able people of the world will work as volunteers at least one day per year in each of the seven departments.

    After each Monthly World Report, a public opinion survey about the report should be taken, and presented to all Advisors.

    All these activities need people to assist with the practical details.

Monthly World Reports + Peace + Freedom + Good Health + Good Family + Good Education + Good Jobs + Harmony = Prosperity + Happiness

Venezia: Libreria (left), San Theodore Column, Palazzo Ducale, Lion of Venice Column (center) on Riva degli Schiavoni street.

Formula issue 18. Preserving all Advisors' decisions

Description: The objective of this issue is to record all activities of the Advisors, and others from the small World Government, to be available to the people on a website.

Formula solution: People with knowledge and experience in this area will prepare a self-management plan.

Starting day: 1 July 2021

Ending day: continuous

Salary: From 35,700/year

Possibility of improving the solution or give another idea: Yes.

Comments: The decisions must be ready for use by all people. The top 10 Advisers will manage Police and all other Departments. All the activities of all Advisors will be recorded in computers and videos, and on paper, for people to be able to see what they are doing. All Advisors are free to speak about their administrative work, with modesty.

Technical and administrative assistance is needed.

Preservation of management records + Peace + Freedom + Good Health + Good Family + Good Education + Good Jobs + Harmony = Prosperity + Happiness

Formula issue 19. Forget war mentality

Description: The objective of this issue is simply to eliminate the war mentality, in order to help all the people on Earth to live better, peacefully, free, healthy, and prosperous.

Formula solution: People with knowledge and experience in this area will prepare a self-management plan.

Starting day: 1 May 2021

Ending day: continuous

Salary: From $28,000/year

Possibility of improving the solution or give another idea: Yes.

Comments: It is a very important effort, useful for everybody. Advisors (and all the others) cannot declare war, reprisals or capture land or water. Advisors (and all the others) cannot raise and support armies, navy, or any military forces.

Over 60 years ago, in Dwight D. Eisenhower's farewell speech, on January 17, 1961, the former famous Five Star General in the Army, Supreme Commander of the Allied Forces in Europe in World War II, and the 34th President of the United States warned of the dangers of allowing a Military-Industrial Complex to take control: "In the councils of government, we must guard against the acquisition of unwarranted influence, whether sought or unsought, by the military–industrial complex". The Military-Industrial Complex is a term that denotes an interdependent relationship between a nation's military, economy, and politics, and it is valid for all nations.

Teachers and many others need to work really hard to eliminate the war mentality, and to transform it in a happy peace mentality. All people need peace, not war.

The war mentality is so bad, that some name things Para Bellum (Prepare for War), instead of the normal Para Pacem (Prepare for Peace) – the people will shortly address this issue.

No war mentality + Peace + Freedom + Good Health + Good Family + Good Education + Good Jobs + Harmony = Prosperity + Happiness

USA, New York, from Times Square: W 44th St, looking southeast, with Virgil's Real Barbecue restaurant (center red), MetLife Building (center back).

Formula issue 20. Work for the 5 assistants

Description: The objective of this issue is to prepare the 5 assistants for all managers.

Formula solution: People with knowledge and experience in this area will prepare a self-management plan.

Starting day: 1 May 2021

Ending day: continuous

Salary: $62,000/year

Possibility of improving the solution or give another idea: Yes.

Comments: It is a sine qua non requirement to have highly qualified professional to help the government to deliver good services to the population. Each Advisor, and each manager at all levels, will have 5 immediate assistants:
1) a mathematician for finance and all other calculations,
2) a medical doctor for keeping everybody healthy, calm, polite, friendly and optimist,
3) a CEO for good management,
4) an engineer for all practical projects, and
5) a teacher for education, training and related areas.

      The five assistants play a key role, because they are highly qualified professionals, who actually will carry on the practical management of the world.

      The five assistants' integrity, professionalism and friendliness will significantly improve the quality of the world and local governments.

      The five assistants are really the experts. They will assist the Advisors and all levels of management, in order to have an efficient, correct and professional working of the world government at all levels.

All spending proposals from Advisers must be approved by their 5 assistants (doctors, mathematicians, CEOs, engineers and teachers), and must have an already existing funding in the budget.

Obviously, much technical, scientific and advanced managerial help is needed for these assistants.

Excellent 5 management assistants + Peace + Freedom + Good Health + Good Family + Good Education + Good Jobs + Harmony = Prosperity + Happiness

Rome: Accademia Nazionale dei Lincei (1603) in Villa Farnesina (1510). The author was invited to give a lecture here in 1978.

Formula issue 21. Organizing elections for the Honorific World Observer

Description: The objective of this issue is to have quiet and civilized elections for this very special top Management.

Formula solution: People with knowledge and experience in this area will prepare a self-management plan.

Starting day: 1 June 2021

Ending day: 2 weeks after election – periodic job, every 3 years

Salary: From $26,000/year

Possibility of improving the solution or give another idea: Yes.

Comments: Serious attention must be given to this process, because of its special importance. An Honorific World Observer will be quietly elected by direct vote – starting, for example, 1st September 2022 - for only one 3 years term, with the main duty to observe that the top 10 Advisers efficiently perform their duties, and keep their words – if they don't, they will be changed. For managers and for everybody else, keeping their word is a serious and strict requirement.

The Honorific World Observer has this responsibility for the top 10 Advisors, but all people will pay attention to this. Words must become again important and respected.

Honorific World Observer election + Peace + Freedom + Good Health + Good Family + Good Education + Good Jobs + Harmony = Prosperity + Happiness

Venere (Venus) Italica, 1810, by Antonio Canova (1757 – 1822, aged 65, sculptor from Venezia), a carved Carrara marble sculpture, 1.75 m, commissioned by Napoleon Bonaparte (1769 – 1821, aged 52).

Formula issue 22. Maintenance of the World Government

Description: The objective of this issue is to help with the logistics for the World Government in order to work better.

Formula solution: People with knowledge and experience in this area will prepare a self-management plan.

Starting day: 1 May 2021

Ending day: continuous

Salary: From $27,000/year

Possibility of improving the solution or give another idea: Yes.

Comments: The World Government needs to be very efficient and economic – all people want this plus peace, freedom, good health, harmony and prosperity.

The World Government will have only 7 Departments, and there are some other important details:

All the employees of the World Government are temporary, and must reapply for their positions every year.

There is no need for unions.

The World Government will be limited to:

1) the Office of the Honorific Observer (less than 10 employees),
2) the Office of the top ten Advisors (less than 100 employees), and
3) 7 small departments.

Good maintenance for the World Government is a high priority activity.

Good working of the World Government + Peace + Freedom + Good Health + Good Family + Good Education + Good Jobs + Harmony = Prosperity + Happiness

Formula issue 23. Assist the 7 World Government Departments

Description: The objective of this issue is to provide specific maintenance work for the World Government Departments.

Formula solution: People with knowledge and experience in this area will prepare a self-management plan.

Starting day: 1 May 2021

Ending day: continuous

Salary: From $36,000/year

Possibility of improving the solution or give another idea: Yes.

Comments: It is a matter of common sense – the World Government needs good maintenance and improvements, in order to have for all people peace, freedom, good health, harmony and prosperity.
   The World Government will have these 7 small departments:

- Tax Department

- Collects taxes of 15% of the income of people and revenue of companies.

- The Manager of the Tax Department is appointed for a three-year term by the World 10 Advisers.

- The number of employees must be under 50,000, with excellent computers, and advanced software.

68

Friendly and correct Tax Department + Peace + Freedom + Good Health + Good Family + Good Education + Good Jobs + Harmony = Prosperity + Happiness

Roma in 2011: the author (68) is at Pantheon (126 AD) and the Fontana del Pantheon in Piazza della Rotonda. Commissioned in 27 BC by Marcus Agrippa (63 BC -12 BC), and rebuilt by Emperor Hadrian (76–138, Emperor 117-138), in about 126.

- Treasury

Treasury will control all the financial issues, including:
- antitrust
- fiscal service
- financial cooperation
- financing bank
- world reserve system
- world budget using only revenue, no borrowing, and spending only on strict necessary needs
– all the budgets, at all levels, will have a 2% surplus, which will be returned to the taxpayers
- register of all government papers and activities
- archives and records
- assist all people to have savings accounts for old age (the old age will be starting around 70), and 10% of their income should automatically go to their savings accounts. For those unable to work, their doctors and mathematicians will decide case by case.
- bankruptcies, in general, will be discouraged, and when strict necessary, will be analyzed and solved, case by case, by the doctors, mathematicians and CEOs who worked with the people who asked the bankruptcy.
- encourage all families to assist their parents, grandparents, and great-grandparents.
- housing finance
- housing for all people
- no homelessness
- consumer financial protection
- pensions
- privacy
- current social security until replaced by personal savings
- personnel Formula solution
- general services for the world government
- each the 10 regions will receive 2.5% of the world taxes - at least 30% of the money will be sent to villages and cities.
- each of the 100 sub-regions will receive 0.25% of the world taxes. At least 40% of the money will be sent to villages and cities.

- The World Central Bank will include all current central banks – starting, for example, on May 1ˢᵗ, 2023.
- The Special Credit Card (SCC) will be issued by the World Central Bank.
- Advisors will create a new world currency, named, for example, "coin", and all the other currencies will be exchanged for coins. The World Central Bank will implement the details.
- The counterfeiting and all other bad things, which some sick people do, will be medically treated (in specialized medical institutions when necessary), and those who did bad things will pay all the expenses, and will reimburse the victims. Victims will always be very protected, and helped to recover the losses from the attackers.

Solid Treasury + Peace + Freedom + Good Health + Good Family + Good Education + Good Jobs + Harmony = Prosperity + Happiness

London: The northwest façade of the Old Vic Theatre (1818, 1871, 1902, 1927, 1938, 1950, 1960, 1963, 1985, 2003, 1067 capacity), on the corner of The Cut and Waterloo Rd., a traditional playhouse with big name actors (Laurence Olivier (1907-1989)) and top directors.

- People Assistance Department

It will assist people in general, including:
- parent assistance
- dispute resolution
- in very simple disputes or culpa levis (ordinary negligence, like late payments, etc.), one single assistant will decide within minutes, and all people will go back to work
- census every 5 years
- election assistance every 20 months
 - special credit cards
- people protection against abuses from anybody
- completely eliminate corruption, organized crime and drug trafficking
- all people in the world will remain in their places, and the improvements will come to them. Those who want to move to other places, will need first a special invitation from at least 10 people (not family related) where they want to move.
- all the Tribunals and related areas will be transformed in people assistance services, based on friendliness, collaboration and goodwill.
- It is well understood that no excessive bail will be required, no excessive fines imposed, no cruel and unusual punishments applied, but, at the same time, it is well understood that a person who did a bad thing will receive the necessary corrective medical treatment, and will reimburse all people who suffered damages, and the medical treatment. The victims will always receive special attention.
- Nobility (King, Prince, etc.) could continue to exist in some places, but they should not interfere with activities of the Advisors, and actually should help them.
- food safety
- trash & recycling
- free commerce
- jobs assistance
- postal service
- labor safety and harmonious relations
- land, water

- volunteers
- fitness, sport, tourism
- 10 world holidays: the normal 4 Earth events (2 solstices (around 21 June, around 21 December), and 2 equinoxes (around 21 May, around 21 September), Mother's Day on 1st May, Father's Day on 6 August, Children's Day on 6 November, Grandparents' Day on 6 February, and 2 optional days (like Thanksgiving or a Religious Day (Christmas), and New Year).

Very dedicated People Assistance Department + Peace + Freedom + Good Health + Good Family + Good Education + Good Jobs + Harmony = Prosperity + Happiness

Boston: 3 Dec 2009, from Harvard Medical School looking northeast to the Avenue Louis Pasteur (1822-1895, French microbiologist).

- Medical Department

It will manage all medical and healthcare related areas, including:
- human services
- conflict resolution
- families, children, elderly
- medicine approval
- disease control and prevention
- medical doctors and assistants will make regular home visits, at least once a year, to all people, to keep them healthy, and to prevent illnesses.
- medical research: cancer, heart, lung, blood, arthritis, surgical robotics, connected computers for healthcare, etc.
- healthy homes, streets, stores, working places, etc.
- healthy aging
- all misunderstandings, disagreements or conflicts of any nature will be treated by medical personnel (with police help when strict necessary), until all is back to normal.
- no prisons are necessary, only specialized medical institutions (in simple cases, the places where the treated people live can be used, with the necessary limitations and surveillance)
- If a person X is considered that did a bad thing, X will have, within 3 days, a discussion with one or more doctors and other assistants, and will be informed of the nature and cause of the bad thing; including witnesses against and for him. Then a decision will be taken within other 3 days, by a group of doctors and other assistants. Victims of bad people will always have priority to discuss their problems with one or more doctors and other assistants, and quick decisions will be taken within 3 days, by a group of doctors and other assistants. Protection of victims has always priority.
- in order to better know the world government, to help it, and, especially, to improve it, all able people of the world will work as volunteers at least one day per year in the local facility of this department, which will have a special office for managing this volunteer work.

– all people will have government medical insurance, and they can also have private medical insurance
– there will be doctors working for the government 100%, or only part-time, or having only private practice, all with reasonable salaries and fees.
– there will be government pharmaceutical institutions and private pharmaceutical companies, offering reasonable priced medicines, without advertising to the general public.

Well-equipped Medical Department + Peace + Freedom + Good Health + Good Family + Good Education + Good Jobs + Harmony = Prosperity + Happiness

USA, Boston: 3 Dec 2009, the northeast façade of the Harvard Medical School Anno Domini 1904, founded in 1782, the graduate medical school of Harvard University, 1660 students, acceptance rate 3.7%.

- Police

Police will provide assistance for:
- accidents
- disasters
- complete elimination of nuclear, chemical and biological arms, firearms and explosives
Ronald Reagan, State of the Union Address, 1984: "A nuclear war cannot be won and must never be fought. The only value, in our two nations possessing nuclear weapons, is to make sure they will never be used. But then would it not be better to do away with them entirely.
- world complete security
- world cooperation
- conflict reduction and resolution
- investigations
- emergency assistance
- training
- delinquency prevention in general, and especially juvenile
- protection of Advisors, important government buildings, etc.
- extended surveillance and reconnaissance to prevent bad events
- fire protection
- volunteers to help police
- police will be present at public meetings, services, shows, etc., in order to protect the public
- public order
- ensuring traffic safety
- completely eliminate corruption, organized crime and drug trafficking
- movement of people based on civilized rules
- assist and protect those who have encountered violence
- World Police and specialists from the former United Nations and Interpol will be ready and very mobile for urgent and special operations, when they are needed.
- Police will be the only department which will have some small arms, in order to stop some very bad people (who are very sick).

- a small manufacturing and maintenance of arms unit will be part of the Police Department, under strict control.
- Police will work with medical personnel, mathematicians, CEOs, engineers, teachers and others, to make sure that all the people on the Planet are in good mental health, in order to prevent bad situations. This is also a major responsibility of all Advisors.
- prevention of bad events
- The Advisors will allocate the necessary budget for Police, and Police will assist people in need.

Kind and helpful Police + Peace + Freedom + Good Health + Good Family + Good Education + Good Jobs + Harmony = Prosperity + Happiness

Mount Washington Resort, Bretton Woods, New Hampshire, USA, where the United Nations Monetary and Financial Conference took place in July 1944.

- Education Department

- Over 2 billions of children in the world will get a solid peace-oriented education, to give a solid peace-oriented foundation for a good, free, peaceful and prosperous life.
- Education is very important – teachers will work with parents and grandparents, to educate the children to leave healthy in a sustainable peace, liberty and prosperity.
- Discipline must be strict, and those who do not behave properly, will get medical assistance.
- The world will have 4 school levels (SLs) of education:
SL1 – Kindergarten – 2 years: age 5 and 6
SL2 – Primary School – 4 years: age 7, 8, 9 and 10
SL3 – Secondary School – 3 years: age 11, 12 and 13
SL4 – High School or Vocational School – 4 years: age 14, 15, 16 and 17
- A World Library will include the Library of Congress and all the other great libraries – they will remain where they are now, but will be digitally interconnected, and accessible from any place in the world.
- adult education: technical, career
- training for employment
- Formula solution training
- post high school education
- peace education
- world constitution education

        Enthusiastic Education Department + Peace + Freedom + Good Health + Good Family + Good Education + Good Jobs + Harmony = Prosperity + Happiness

USA, Boston, 3 Dec 2009, from Avenue Louis Pasteur (1822-1895, French microbiologist), Boston Public Latin School (1635, Schola Latina Bostoniensis, the oldest and the first public exam school in the U.S.).

- Science & Technology Department.

It will help in the areas of:
- mathematics
- statistics
- science
- technology
- Algorithmic Governance will be an essential tool for a better and impartial governing of the world, used by the Advisers elected by people. Mathematicians from all countries will work to improve the Algorithmic Governance, to better serve the people.
- cyberspace complete security will be achieved and strictly maintained
- information systems
- computer services
- Internet
- scientific cooperation
- economic development at the world level
- infrastructure improvement and maintenance at the world level
- innovation and improvements in all areas, at the world level
- transportation at the world level
- safety
- security
- aviation
- highway
- cars
- railroads without noise
- maritime administration
- logistics
- strategic planning at the world level
- public works
- fleet maintenance
- standards: weights, measures, etc.
- research at the world level
- risk analysis
- laboratories
- engineering

- communications at the world level
- telecommunications
- networks
- peaceful nuclear energy use at the world level
- safety
- waste
- electrical power
- oceanic analysis at the world level
- atmospheric analysis at the global level
- meteorological service and prognosis at the global level
- world resources analysis
- sustainable use of world resources
- geographical and geological activity
- product safety at the global level
- hazardous material and chemical safety
- government broadcasting (radio, tv, Internet, newspaper, etc.) including news, scientific and technical information
- private broadcasting will continue, but the world government must be able to directly inform the people, without intermediaries
- space exploration and expansion at the world level – very important for the future
- patent and trademark
- intellectual rights
- all government work, which can be done by private companies, will be contracted with the best and reasonably priced private companies. At the same time, the government should always have competitive services for people – from plumbing and electrical help, to mortgage and buying or selling a house.

Inventive and creative Science & Technology Department + Peace + Freedom + Good Health + Good Family + Good Education + Good Jobs + Harmony = Prosperity + Happiness

Formula issue 24. Supervise the elections

Description: The objective of this issue is to provide good and impartial administration of all the elections.

Formula solution: People with knowledge and experience in this area will prepare a self-management plan.

Starting day: 1 May 2021

Ending day: continuous

Salary: From $27,000/year

Possibility of improving the solution or give another idea: Yes.

Comments: Obviously, calm and friendly elections are needed, and their good administration is essential. Political ad spending is over $6.7 B per election; therefore, people's money is transferred to local TV – not good for people. Elections, with zero spending, will be every 20 months.

The Advisers will be elected every 20 months for one term only. If an Adviser X was elected for a term T1, then the next term T2 will have another Advisor Y. For the next term T3, X can be elected again, but the next term T4 will have a new Adviser, and so on. All levels of Advisers (minimum age 25 years) can be elected, not consecutively, at most 4 times (maximum 80 months = 6 years and 8 months).

Advisers should have exceptional results obtained from their work, and based on these results, plus modesty, moderation, good character, friendliness, sharp mind, wisdom, good morals, and intense desire to help people, they will be elected, without any campaigning, publicity, fundraising, donations, debates, propaganda, political parties, advertising, or similar activities.

There will be use of advanced digital technology, which opens up entirely new opportunities for developing direct elections, and public control of the institutions, improving the transparency of the election procedure, and taking into account the interests and opinions of each voter (over the age of 21, who are not in a special medical institution for bad behavior or for mental health).

Calm, joyful and zero money elections + Peace + Freedom + Good Health + Good Family + Good Education + Good Jobs + Harmony = Prosperity + Happiness

Italy, Rome (753 BC), Villa Borghese (1630), Lake Garden, from Viale del Lago, Tempio di Esculapio (1786, Temple of Asclepius (god of medicine, healing, rejuvenation and physicians)) on artificial island; on front, in Greek "To Asclepius the savior".

Formula issue 25. Verify the qualifications

Description: The objective of this issue is to check the qualifications of those who want to run for elections.

Formula solution: People with knowledge and experience in this area will prepare a self-management plan.

Starting day: 1 May 2021

Ending day: continuous

Salary: From $40,000/year

Possibility of improving the solution or give another idea: Yes.

Comments: It is very important to have well qualified elected managers. The Election Commission of 110 representatives from the 10 regions and from the 100 sub-regions, elected separately for 5 years, will have to examine the qualifications of all the candidates for Advisers, and for other senior management positions. Unqualified candidates will be asked to improve their qualifications, and then to try again later.

It is important to refresh the management, and to bring new people to help the big family of 7.7 B people. The older generations, who performed well, will be retained in important roles, because experience and maturity count very much. At least two months before the retirement, they will kindly be asked to transfer their expertise to the younger generation. Even after retirement, they will occasionally be invited to share their expertise.

In every election, with every winner, will be other two for number 2 and number 3. The number 2 and number 3 for each management position will be used when number 1 is not available (vacation, sick, etc.). They will constantly work for number 1, helping to solve urgent problems for the people.

Good elections are essential for the future.

There has been a tendency to make elections conflict generating events, with lots of propaganda, false information, heavy donations, unpolite confrontations, bully fundraising, hostile political parties and organizations, unlimited power ambitions, etc.

This will be completely changed into clean, friendly elections, in which people choose between leaders with outstanding results, plus talent to lead people to peace and freedom, modesty, moderation, good character, friendliness, sharp mind, wisdom, good morals, and intense desire to help people – no campaigning, no publicity, no fundraising, no donations, no debates, no propaganda, no political parties, no advertising or similar activities.

The Election Commission, after examining many good candidates, will invite the best to participate in very friendly elections.

Only non-dictatorial candidates for the calm, joyful and zero money elections + Peace + Freedom + Good Health + Good Family + Good Education + Good Jobs + Harmony = Prosperity + Happiness

Formula issue 26. Referendum assistance

Description: The objective of this issue is to administer all referenda.

Formula solution: People with knowledge and experience in this area will prepare a self-management plan.

Starting day: 1 February 2021

Ending day: continuous

Salary: From $27,000/year

Possibility of improving the solution or give another idea: Yes.

Comments: Referendum is a necessity for good government. An electronic world referendum will be organized every three months. The main questions will be:
1. Are you satisfied with the Government?
2. What Government work is good?
3. What Government work is not good?
4: Suggestions for improvement:

Within two months after each referendum, the Government will respond to the people. Based on the suggestions received, new pro-people rules will be replacing some old rules.

Frequent referenda + Peace + Freedom + Good Health + Good Family + Good Education + Good Jobs + Harmony = Prosperity + Happiness

Formula issue 27. Complete disarmament verification

Description: The objective of this issue is to carefully monitor the complete disarmament on the Planet.

Formula solution: Specialized police departments, scientists, and other specialists in this area will prepare a self-management plan.

Starting day: 1 May 2021

Ending day: continuous

Salary: From $60,000/year

Possibility of improving the solution or give another idea: Yes.

Comments: It is a matter of common sense – all people want complete disarmament, peace, freedom, good health, harmony and prosperity on the planet.
There will be no arms at all:
Arms will not exist anymore, and only the police will have some small arms. Those who want arms for hunting or sport, will borrow them from police stations, with proper documents, rules and payments.
All military units will become strong civilian organizations, working to improve the quality of life for everybody.
A continuous verification and monitoring will be implemented, the make sure that the world finally achieved complete disarmament.
With so many arms now in private hands, it will take a strong effort to collect and destroy all the arms, but it will be done.

Complete disarmament + Peace + Freedom + Good Health + Good Family + Good Education + Good Jobs + Harmony = Prosperity + Happiness

Formula issue 28. Census assistance

Description: The objective of this issue is administering the census every 5 years.

Formula solution: People with knowledge and experience in this area will prepare a self-management plan.

Starting day: 1 October 2023

Ending day: 31 December 2023

Salary: From $22,000/year every 5 years

Possibility of improving the solution or give another idea: Yes.

Comments: Census is necessary to better assist the people. It is also useful for delimitations, special cards, etc. A census will take place every 5 years – starting, for example, on October 1st, 2023 - and all people will receive a special credit card (SCC), with their photo and other personal data. The delimitations between regions, and between sub-regions, will be adjusted by the census.

Accurate census + Peace + Freedom + Good Health + Good Family + Good Education + Good Jobs + Harmony = Prosperity + Happiness

Formula issue 29. Special Credit Cards assistance

Description: The objective of this issue is to help with the administration of the special credit cards for all people.

Formula solution: People with knowledge and experience in this area will prepare a self-management plan.

Starting day: 1 May 2021

Ending day: continuous

Salary: From $26,000/year

Possibility of improving the solution or give another idea: Yes.

Comments: It is a matter of common sense – all people need these cards for many things. The special credit card (SCC) will be used to buy everything, to identify for voting (no bureaucratic registration for voting – all people are automatically registered voters), for census, for travel, for medical assistance, etc.

The current private credit cards will continue to work as usual.

The changes of the delimitations between regions, and also sub-regions, will be inputted on these cards, and no other work is needed.

Special Credit Cards for all + Peace + Freedom + Good Health + Good Family + Good Education + Good Jobs + Harmony = Prosperity + Happiness

Formula issue 30. Help for virus control and elimination

Description: The objective of this issue is a major medical effort for virus control and elimination.

Formula solution: Medical specialists, and people with knowledge and experience in this area will prepare a self-management plan.

Starting day: 1 May 2021

Ending day: continuous

Salary: From $49,000/year

Possibility of improving the solution or give another idea: Yes.

Comments: It is a matter of common sense – all people want good health, peace, freedom, harmony and prosperity. People are something sacred for people. The enemies of the people on Earth are not other people, but viruses, microbes, bad bacteria and hundreds of deadly illnesses – all people on Earth will work together against these real enemies for all of us. The planet must be healthy.

Virus control on Peaceful Terra + Peace + Freedom + Good Health + Good Family + Good Education + Good Jobs + Harmony = Prosperity + Happiness

Italy, Roma (753 BC, one of the oldest occupied cities in Europe, called Roma Aeterna (The Eternal City) and Caput Mundi (Capital of the World)), southeast of Piazza del Popolo (1822, by Giuseppe Valadier, inside the northern gate in the Aurelian Walls, the Porta Flaminia, now called the Porta del Popolo), near Via del Babuino (opened in 1525 as the Via Paolina) and the church Santa Maria in Montesanto (1679, begun by Rainaldi and completed by Bernini and Fontana), the statue of the Goddess of Abundance.

Formula issue 31. Working for Non-violence implementation

Description: The objective of this issue is simply to eliminate all forms of violence.

Formula solution: People with knowledge and experience in this area will prepare a self-management plan.

Starting day: 1 May 2021

Ending day: continuous

Salary: From $33,000/year

Possibility of improving the solution or give another idea: Yes.

Comments: It is a matter of common sense – all people want non-violence, peace, freedom, good health, harmony and prosperity. Non-violence is directly related to medical assistance. Non-violence is a strict requirement for all activities on Earth. The first rule for everybody on Earth comes from the Hippocratic Oath: Primum non nocere - first do not harm.
        Plenty of jobs are in this area.

        Elimination of violence + Peace + Freedom + Good Health + Good Family + Good Education + Good Jobs + Harmony = Prosperity + Happiness

Formula issue 32. Working to help doctors

Description: The objective of this issue is simply to improve people's heath by having regular doctors' home visits.

Formula solution: People with knowledge and experience in this area will prepare a self-management plan.

Starting day: 1 May 2021

Ending day: continuous

Salary: From $39,000/year

Possibility of improving the solution or give another idea: Yes.

Comments: It is a matter of common sense – all people want good health, peace, freedom, harmony and prosperity. Home visits will be a real joy! Medical doctors and assistants will make regular home visits to all people, to keep them healthy, and to prevent illnesses.
There are many jobs in this area.

Regular doctors' home visits + Peace + Freedom + Good Health + Good Family + Good Education + Good Jobs + Harmony = Prosperity + Happiness

Formula issue 33. Working for truth promotion

Description: The objective of this issue is simply to return to the truth.

Formula solution: People with knowledge and experience in this area will prepare a self-management plan.

Starting day: 1 May 2021

Ending day: continuous

Salary: $36,000/year

Possibility of improving the solution or give another idea: Yes.

Comments: Truth is needed everywhere, and many people are needed to help. Truth and collaboration are basic elements. People need only truth in order to create a long term peaceful and harmonious society. If someone lies – medical treatment will follow.
     If 7 billions of people say a wrong thing, it's still a wrong thing.

     Truth + Peace + Freedom + Good Health + Good Family + Good Education + Good Jobs + Harmony = Prosperity + Happiness

France, Paris: The Panthéon (1758 - 1790, 83 m height, mausoleum in the Latin Quarter in Paris, modeled on the Pantheon (25 BC, 126 AD) in Rome), seen from Rue Soufflot.

Formula issue 34. Working for freedom implementation

Description: The objective of this issue is simply to have freedom for everybody.

Formula solution: People with knowledge and experience in this area will prepare a self-management plan.

Starting day: 1 May 2021

Ending day: continuous

Salary: From $37,000/year

Possibility of improving the solution or give another idea: Yes.

Comments: Freedom is a fundamental requirement on Earth. It is well understood that this freedom refers to doing good things in a civilized manner, not for war, for violence or similar bad things, which are against the wellbeing of the people. Freedom goes hand in hand with responsibility. People can assemble peacefully only.

Many people will have to diligently work on this issue, and it will be a great success.

Thomas Jefferson (1743 - 1826) - "Rightful liberty is unobstructed action according to our will within limits drawn around us by the equal rights of others. I do not add 'within the limits of the law' because the law is often but the tyrant's will, and always so when it violates the right of an individual."

Freedom + Peace + Good Health + Good Family + Good Education + Good Jobs + Harmony = Prosperity + Happiness

Formula issue 35. Working for economy improvement

Description: The objective of this issue is simply to have a better economy for all.

Formula solution: People with knowledge and experience in this area will prepare a self-management plan.

Starting day: 1 May 2021

Ending day: continuous

Salary: From $28,000/year

Possibility of improving the solution or give another idea: Yes.

Comments: The free-market economy is not perfect, but it will be improved. All people will have the option to choose between friendly private services, and friendly government services. Independent assistants and monitors will make sure that there are no abuses. Sine qua non requirements for happiness are morality and free market.

Self-improvement is essential - Marcus Aurelius (26 April 121, Rome, Italy – 17 March 180, (58.9) Vindobona, now in Austria, Roman emperor for 19 years from 161 to 180 and a Stoic philosopher. one of the great rulers of the Roman Empire), sets forth a series of self-reflective essays intended as a guide for his own self-improvement

14 February – World day of love and friendship.

Good economy + Peace + Freedom + Good Health + Good Family + Good Education + Good Jobs + Harmony = Prosperity + Happiness

Italy, Vatican, Basilica Papale di San Pietro (1506), an ancient Egyptian obelisk (center right, of red granite, 25.5 m, 41 m total, from Heliopolis, Egypt, 2400 BC, moved by Emperor Augustus in 30 BC to Alexandria, in 37 to Rome, here in 1586).

Formula issue 36. Working for religion collaboration

Description: The objective of this issue is to encourage collaboration between different religions, for the benefit of all people.

Formula solution: People with knowledge and experience in this area will prepare a self-management plan.

Starting day: 1 May 2021

Ending day: continuous

Salary: $40,000/year

Possibility of improving the solution or give another idea: Yes.

Comments: It is a matter of common sense – all people want peace, freedom, good health, harmony and prosperity. Competent people will work with great attention in order to find and explain the many common points in all religions – peace, family, love, non-violence, helping each other, etc.

Religion collaboration + Peace + Freedom + Good Health + Good Family + Good Education + Good Jobs + Harmony = Prosperity + Happiness

Formula issue 37. Working for government improvement

Description: The objective of this issue is simply to make the World Government better.

Formula solution: People with knowledge and experience in this area will prepare a self-management plan.

Starting day: 1 May 2021

Ending day: continuous

Salary: $34,000/year

Possibility of improving the solution or give another idea: Yes.

Comments: It is a matter of common sense – all people want better government. People of course can petition the small Word Government, and can change it anytime, if it does not perform as expected.

A great number of jobs will be in this area.

Better Government + Peace + Freedom + Good Health + Good Family + Good Education + Good Jobs + Harmony = Prosperity + Happiness

Formula issue 38. Working for balanced budget

Description: The objective of this issue is simply to balance the budget, like every good family does.

Formula solution: People with knowledge and experience in this area will prepare a self-management plan.

Starting day: 1 May 2021

Ending day: continuous

Salary: From $38,000/year

Possibility of improving the solution or give another idea: Yes.

Comments: All budgets will have surplus of 2% - there will be a strict application of the Latin aphorism: "Sumptus censum ne superset" (Let not your spending exceed your income).
    Many will have good jobs in this area.

    Balanced budget + Peace + Freedom + Good Health + Good Family + Good Education + Good Jobs + Harmony = Prosperity + Happiness

Formula issue 39. Working for errors elimination

Description: The objective of this issue is simply to eliminate the many thousands of errors, which accumulated over the years.

Formula solution: People with knowledge and experience in this area will prepare a self-management plan.

Starting day: 1 May 2021

Ending day: continuous

Salary: From $35,000/year

Possibility of improving the solution or give another idea: Yes.

Comments: It is a burning issue - correcting errors is a permanent duty for everybody - Darwin (circa 140 years ago) said "To kill an error is as good a service as, and sometimes even better than, the establishing of a new truth or fact."

People make errors all the time – including the error of blaming something else for their errors. Corrective actions are necessary.

Error elimination + Peace + Freedom + Good Health + Good Family + Good Education + Good Jobs + Harmony = Prosperity + Happiness

Formula issue 40. Working to promote kindness

Description: The objective of this issue is simply to always have kindness for everybody.

Formula solution: Teachers, and people with knowledge and experience in this area will prepare a self-management plan.

Starting day: 1 May 2021

Ending day: continuous

Salary: From $30,000/year

Possibility of improving the solution or give another idea: Yes.

Comments: Kindness is a necessity – it is a requirement for everybody. Seneca (circa 1,960 years ago) said "Wherever there is a human being, there is an opportunity for a kindness." This is a fundamental idea which must be constantly applied.

Therefore, kind people will have many jobs in this area.

Kindness + Peace + Freedom + Good Health + Good Family + Good Education + Good Jobs + Harmony = Prosperity + Happiness

Belgium, 19 March 1978, Bruxelles (990, population 1.1 M), from Grand Place looking to the northwest façade of a classical building.

Formula issue 41. Working for Government mobility

Description: The objective of this issue is to have a very mobile government, which goes to people, not vice-versa.

Formula solution: People with knowledge and experience in this area will prepare a self-management plan.

Starting day: 1 May 2021

Ending day: continuous

Salary: From $38,000/year

Possibility of improving the solution or give another idea: Yes.

Comments: The more mobility the government has, the better people will be served. All levels of government will be highly mobile - changing of the capitals for the 10 regions, and for the 100 sub-regions, etc. It is necessary to move the government close to the people, to be able to quickly solve the local problems.

Obviously, many jobs will be around.

Government mobility + Peace + Freedom + Good Health + Good Family + Good Education + Good Jobs + Harmony = Prosperity + Happiness

Formula issue 42. Work to have friendly world police

Description: The objective of this issue is to have a very friendly world police.

Formula solution: People with knowledge and experience in this area will prepare a self-management plan.

Starting day: 1 May 2021

Ending day: continuous

Salary: From $38,000/year

Possibility of improving the solution or give another idea: Yes.

Comments: It is a matter of common sense – all people want peace, freedom, good health, harmony, prosperity, and friendly police to help them when necessary. Police will help people everywhere. The United Nations will change in 2-3 years (for example, by 2024) into World Police and Assistance Organization (WPAO), to help local police in case of big natural disasters or big accidents, and will report to the top 10 Advisers. The police will be located in all capitals, and help the locals. When an emergency appears, they will quickly move to solve the emergency.

The police powers will be limited, and they will know and be friend with all the people in their jurisdiction – this is the key element of a civilized and peaceful Earth.

Police will be people's friends everywhere, and they will always help people.

Prevention of bad events is the main objective of everybody. If a bad event occurs, the police and their assistants will eliminate the consequences, reestablish the normal situation, and determine why the bad event occurred, in order to improve their activity, and prevent such bad events in the future.

In order to prevent bad things, the police, doctors and their assistants will be in permanent contact with all the people, by visiting them, phone calls, e-mails, tele-videos, and mail, to keep everybody calm and happy.

Many jobs will be available for this important objective.

Friendly world police + Peace + Freedom + Good Health + Good Family + Good Education + Good Jobs + Harmony = Prosperity + Happiness

USA, Cleveland, 9 August 1979, The Fountain of Eternal Life, in front of the old Cleveland Board of Education building (1931-2013 (82 years), the author worked here in 1980-1985; from 2016 in this transformed building is Drury Plaza Hotel).

Formula issue 43. Working for non-stop Government

Description: The objective of this issue is to assist the government to work continuously.

Formula solution: People with knowledge and experience in this area will prepare a self-management plan.

Starting day: 1 May 2021

Ending day: continuous

Salary: From $25,000/year

Possibility of improving the solution or give another idea: Yes.

Comments: It is only normal to have always someone in the government to help. About 66% of the Government will always be working somewhere on the Earth - if people need help, they can always call the Government. Non-stop working of all world government departments – especially medical, police, emergency, volunteers – will be carefully organized.

To help this process, many jobs will be around.

Non-stop World Government + Peace + Freedom + Good Health + Good Family + Good Education + Good Jobs + Harmony = Prosperity + Happiness

108

Italy, 12 May 1978, Bologna (1000 BC, 140 km^2, elevation 54 m, metro population 1 M, the capital and largest city of the Emilia-Romagna region in Northern Italy, with the oldest university in the world, University of Bologna, founded in 1088), west of Piazza di Porta San Donato, from Via Zamboni looking east to the north façade of the Università degli Studi di Bologna, Dipartimento di Matematica, Istituto di Matematica.

Formula issue 44. Working for respect of privacy

Description: The objective of this issue is simply to increase the respect for privacy.

Formula solution: People with knowledge and experience in this area will prepare a self-management plan.

Starting day: 1 May 2021

Ending day: continuous

Salary: From $24,000/year

Possibility of improving the solution or give another idea: Yes.

Comments: It is clear that privacy is needed. Privacy of negotiations and discussions are necessary. In order to have serious and constructive discussions and negotiations, they must be private.

Privacy and discipline are necessary for good government work.

Self-discipline is a strict requirement for everybody.

The results will be public and preserved, but not the private discussions.

Good jobs will be available.

Privacy + Peace + Freedom + Good Health + Good Family + Good Education + Good Jobs + Harmony = Prosperity + Happiness

Formula issue 45. Polite Government

Description: The objective of this issue is simply to create a very polite government. Impossible? No! Inevitable? Yes!

Formula solution: People with knowledge and experience in this area will prepare a self-management plan.

Starting day: 1 May 2021

Ending day: continuous

Salary: starting at $27,000/year

Possibility of improving the solution or give another idea: Yes.

Comments: All people want polite government, peace, freedom, good health, harmony and prosperity.

It is a strict requirement for the top managements, and for all others, to be highly civilized, polite, courteous, harmonious and efficient.

Who wants to work for the world government must have good manners.

Harmony in the world starts from the harmony and good manners of the people in the world government.

Because all people on Earth want to live in harmony right now, it will be relatively easy to implement this in one good and civilized country. This may include having small, beautiful and commonly agreed fences around properties, because good fences make good neighbors, and also helps with more privacy.

So, plenty of jobs.

Polite Government + Peace + Freedom + Good Health + Good Family + Good Education + Good Jobs + Harmony = Prosperity + Happiness

Egypt, the upper part of the Great Pyramid of Giza, 2560 BC, 146.5 m.

Japan, 19 Nov 2008, looking south to a blooming tree (left) after the mid of November and the author (65, invited at TDU), near an artesian fountain in the central park from the Inzai (Chiba) campus of Tokyo Denki University (TDU), at sunset; the building to the right is the Library.

Formula issue 46. Working for conflict resolution

Description: The objective of this issue is to eliminate all types of conflicts on Earth.

Formula solution: People with knowledge and experience in this area will prepare a self-management plan.

Starting day: 1 May 2021

Ending day: continuous

Salary: from $24,000/year

Possibility of improving the solution or give another idea: Yes.

Comments: All people want no conflicts, peace, freedom, good health, harmony and prosperity. All conflicts must not only be quickly resolved, but they also must be transformed in friendships. This is very important for long term stability.

The medical personnel and others will work diligently to make sure that disputes are resolved, and then a friendship is developed. Only in this way the situation will become stable. Conflicts will be quickly resolved, and then the corrective medical treatment will include the transformation of hostility and aggressiveness into harmony and friendship.

Dispute resolution is not only Government's obligation, but it will be everybody's duty. There will be professional assistance from medical personnel, police, people assistance specialists, volunteers, religious organizations, and many others, but the bottom line is that everybody must avoid disputes.

Therefore, great jobs for those talented in this area.

Fast dispute resolution + Peace + Freedom + Good Health + Good Family + Good Education + Good Jobs + Harmony = Prosperity + Happiness

Rome (753 BC), Vatican (1929): Piazza di San Pietro (1656 – 1667, Bernini), with Moderno's façade (115 m wide, 46 m high) of the Basilica di San Pietro (1506 – 1626), and an Egyptian obelisk (1250 BC, 25.5 m, total height 40 m), moved here in 1586.

Formula issue 47. Common language and alphabet

Description: The objective of this issue is simply to establish a common language and alphabet.

Formula solution: Teachers and people with knowledge and experience in this area will prepare a self-management plan.

Starting day: 1 May 2021

Ending day: continuous

Salary: from $30,000/year

Possibility of improving the solution or give another idea: Yes.

Comments: It is a matter of common sense – all people want to easily communicate with each other, to have peace, freedom, good health, harmony and prosperity. As a single big, over 7.7 B, family on Earth, all people must be able to communicate easily with each other. For this reason, a common language and alphabet on Earth are needed. Because English is a de facto common language now, it will be taken as the basis of the world language, let's call it Mundo, which will be taught in all schools, and used in the world government. All the other languages will continue as secondary languages. The same is true for the Latin alphabet, which will be used everywhere, with other alphabets as secondary. The teachers will have a very significant role in implementing this Global Task, and many others will have good jobs helping the teachers.

Common language and alphabet + Peace + Freedom + Good Health + Good Family + Good Education + Good Jobs + Harmony = Prosperity + Happiness

USA, Arizona, Tucson (1877, elevation 728 m, population 530,000), May 1979, (the author, 35.5, was invited at the University of Arizona (1885, academic staff 3,000, students 43,000)).

Italy, ruins of Pompeii (650 BC, in 79 covered by ash), the northwest part of Theatrum Odeon (80 BC, for music and poetry).

Formula issue 48. Increasing global wealth

Description: The objective of this issue is to increase the global wealth.

Formula solution: People with knowledge and experience in this area will prepare a self-management plan.

Starting day: 1 May 2021

Ending day: continuous

Salary: From $50,000/year

Possibility of improving the solution or give another idea: Yes.

Comments: Obviously, all the global wealth will be carefully used only for peace, freedom and prosperity for all. The 2018 Global Wealth Report from Credit Suisse shows that the total global wealth has reached $317 trillions (circa $41,000/person), which is encouraging, and all this wealth must be increased and used only for peace. To increase the global wealth, everybody will be encouraged to improve everything, to create, to innovate, to research, to develop, to produce new and better products for all people, etc. It is a major responsibility of the Government to increase the global wealth, and to train those in need, to have better working abilities and opportunities. Plenty of great jobs for innovators, researchers, creators, developers, etc.

Big global wealth + Peace + Freedom + Good Health + Good Family + Good Education + Good Jobs + Harmony = Prosperity + Happiness

Paris - The central part of the façade of L'Opéra de Paris (1875): composers Daniel Auber (1782–1871, left), Ludwig van Beethoven (1770–1827, second), Wolfgang Amadeus Mozart (1756–1791, center) and Gaspare Spontini (1774–1851, right).

Formula issue 49. Working on bureaucracy elimination

Description: The objective of this issue is to eliminate bureaucracy.

Formula solution: Experts interested in the elimination of bureaucracy will prepare a self-management plan.

Starting day: 1 May 2021

Ending day: continuous

Salary: Starting at $27,000/year

Possibility of improving the solution or give another idea: Yes.

Comments: The goal is no bureaucracy whatsoever. In a well-organized country, with all people working together in harmony, this can be accomplished in several years.
Constant attention will be focused on avoiding duplication at all levels of the world government – there must be continuous collaboration between all levels, to prevent duplication, and to eliminate it, if it was found.
Numerous jobs for people interested in the elimination of bureaucracy.

No bureaucracy + Peace + Freedom + Good Health + Good Family + Good Education + Good Jobs + Harmony = Prosperity + Happiness

Formula issue 50. Working for corruption eradication

Description: The objective of this issue is to eradicate corruption.

Formula solution: Experts interested in the elimination of corruption will prepare a self-management plan.

Starting day: 1 May 2021

Ending day: continuous

Salary: Starting at $28,000.

Possibility of improving the solution or give another idea: Yes.

Comments: Everybody can have a good job to work really hard to completely eliminate corruption, organized crime and drug trafficking. Those involved in such bad activities will receive corrective medical treatment, until they become good working people.

No corruption + Peace + Freedom + Good Health + Good Family + Good Education + Good Jobs + Harmony = Prosperity + Happiness

Formula issue 51. Working to encourage savings

Description: The objective of this issue is simply to encourage savings.

Formula solution: Experts who know to balance family budgets, and want to help others, will prepare a self-management plan.

Starting day: 1 May 2021

Ending day: continuous

Salary: From $30,000/year

Possibility of improving the solution or give another idea: Yes.

Comments: A world reserve system will be created.

Each government department will have some reserves for special situations (natural disasters, big accidents), and the banks will also have good financial reserves.

All people can have a good job to encourage other people to save some money in banks which pay 5% interest.

Good savings + Peace + Freedom + Good Health + Good Family + Good Education + Good Jobs + Harmony = Prosperity + Happiness

Formula issue 52. Working for Government efficiency

Description: The objective of this issue is to improve government efficiency.

Formula solution: Experts with knowledge and experience in improving government efficiency will prepare a self-management plan.

Starting day: 1 May 2021

Ending day: continuous

Salary: From $40,000/year

Possibility of improving the solution or give another idea: Yes.

Comments: Inspectors will help the Government with the integrity and efficiency issues – always there are ways to improve the work.
Inspectors will give advice regarding integrity and efficiency, and will take corrective actions when necessary.
Plenty of good jobs to improve government efficiency.

Efficient Government + Peace + Freedom + Good Health + Good Family + Good Education + Good Jobs + Harmony = Prosperity + Happiness

Formula issue 53. Family assistance

Description: The objective of this issue is simply to assist all families.

Formula solution: Experts with knowledge and experience in family assistance will prepare a self-management plan.

Starting day: 1 May 2021

Ending day: continuous

Salary: From $36,000/year.

Possibility of improving the solution or give another idea: Yes.

Comments: It is a matter of common sense – all people want healthy families with happy children, peace, freedom, good health, harmony and prosperity.

Because all families need assistance from time to time, and the big 7.7 B family on Earth contains billions of small families, all of them will have the assistance they need – this will be the result of one country well organized and managed.

All people can have great jobs to assist families.

Good family assistance + Peace + Freedom + Good Health + Good Family + Good Education + Good Jobs + Harmony = Prosperity + Happiness

Formula issue 54. Abuse purging

Description: The objective of this issue is to get rid of abuses, which are quite frequent.

Formula solution: Experts who have knowledge and experience in finding, analyzing and correcting abuses will prepare a self-management plan.

Starting day: 1 May 2021

Ending day: continuous

Salary: From $47,000/year.

Possibility of improving the solution or give another idea: Yes.

Comments: It is a demanding effort, after thousands of years of all kinds of abuses, but the abuses will be gone!

Special attention will be given by Advisors to avoid abuses and wrong interpretations of the rules. All assistants (doctors, mathematicians, CEOs, engineers and teachers) will closely monitor all activities, to avoid abuses and wrong interpretations of the rules.

This requirement of not having abuses is demanding – but this is a general job, not only for Government – it is everybody, as part of the big family, we just don't need abuses.

The abuse, in some places, of confiscating the land by some government bureaucrats will be eliminated – the land belongs to the people, not the government.

The abuse, in some places, of having trains, airplanes, and others making unhealthy noises, with the government support, will be eliminated – peoples' health has always priority.

The abuse, in some places, of having to change the clocks twice a year will be eliminated – only the normal local time zones will be used.

If abuses are observed, they will be immediately reported to the Government, and corrected, in general, by the People Assistance Department, which will have personnel, including medical assistants, to analyze and promptly solve the abuses. The abusers will undergo corrective medical treatment, and will pay significant financial charges.

As we can see, there are plenty of good jobs for this demanding task of eliminating abuses.

No abuses + Peace + Freedom + Good Health + Good Family + Good Education + Good Jobs + Harmony = Prosperity + Happiness

UK, London, The west façade and entrance of Westminster Abbey (960, 1517, Collegiate Church of St Peter at Westminster, Anglican abbey with daily services and coronations since 1066, tower height 69 m).

Formula issue 55. Working for free commerce

Description: The objective of this issue is simply to encourage free commerce.

Formula solution: Experts with knowledge and experience in commerce will prepare a self-management plan.

Starting day: 1 May 2021

Ending day: continuous

Salary: From $25,000/year

Possibility of improving the solution or give another idea: Yes.

Comments: People need intense free commerce.

In one country, with one market, the commerce between the people on Earth will be free of taxes, tariffs, duties, etc. – plenty of jobs for everybody.

Free commerce + Peace + Freedom + Good Health + Good Family + Good Education + Good Jobs + Harmony = Prosperity + Happiness

Formula issue 56. Working for free and responsible speech and press

Description: The objective of this issue is simply to make sure that there is free and responsible speech and press.

Formula solution: Experts with knowledge and experience in free and responsible speech and press will prepare a self-management plan.

Starting day: 1 May 2021

Ending day: continuous

Salary: From $43,000/year.

Possibility of improving the solution or give another idea: Yes.

Comments: People need free and responsible speech and press.

It is expected not to call for war, violence, or similar destructive activities. People want peace, freedom, health, friendship and prosperity.

Good jobs will be available for those qualified for this important Formula issue.

Free and responsible speech and press + Peace + Freedom + Good Health + Good Family + Good Education + Good Jobs + Harmony = Prosperity + Happiness

Italy, 6 April 1978, Pisa, Cattedrale di Pisa (1092, striped-marble, left), Torre di Pisa (August 1173-1372, 55.86 m on the low side, 56.67 m on the high side, white-marble, 296 steps, right).

Formula issue 57. Working for government integrity

Description: The objective of this issue is simply to improve the government integrity.

Formula solution: People with knowledge and experience in government integrity will prepare a self-management plan.

Starting day: 1 May 2021

Ending day: continuous

Salary: From $43,000/year

Possibility of improving the solution or give another idea: Yes.

Comments: A Latin proverb says: "Integrity is the noblest possession". With this in mind, good jobs will be available for those qualified to work on improving the government integrity.

Government integrity + Peace + Freedom + Good Health + Good Family + Good Education + Good Jobs + Harmony = Prosperity + Happiness

Formula issue 58. Working for peaceful assemble

Description: The objective of this issue is simply to assist in organizing peaceful assembly.

Formula solution: Experts with knowledge and experience in organizing peaceful assembly and meetings will prepare a self-management plan.

Starting day: 1 May 2021.

Ending day: continuous.

Salary: From $38,000/year.

Possibility of improving the solution or give another idea: Yes.

Comments: People want peaceful assembly, when needed.

If some disagree with a decision, they can always inform the government, which will respond in 3 days. The discussion will continue with calm and respect, until everything is clarified.

People can assemble peacefully only, with police for help. It is expected not to call for war, violence, or similar destructive activities. People want peace, freedom, health, friendship and prosperity. If some use violence, they will undergo corrective medical treatment, and will pay significant financial fees.

There will be need for people qualified in organizing peaceful assembly and meetings, therefore good jobs for them.

Peaceful assemble + Peace + Freedom + Good Health + Good Family + Good Education + Good Jobs + Harmony = Prosperity + Happiness

Formula issue 59. Helping people to find jobs

Description: The objective of this issue is simply to help people to find jobs.

Formula solution: Experts with knowledge and experience in assisting people to find jobs will prepare a self-management plan.

Starting day: 1 May 2021

Ending day: continuous

Salary: From $37,000/year.

Possibility of improving the solution or give another idea: Yes.

Comments: There will always be plenty of jobs at world minimum wage (assisting other people, for example), and the standard situation will be this: more jobs than available people, so people will choose the jobs they like the most.

Good jobs for those qualified in assisting people to find jobs.

Good jobs + Peace + Freedom + Good Health + Good Family + Good Education + Harmony = Prosperity + Happiness

Formula issue 60. Working for clean and safe streets

Description: The objective of this issue is simply to have clean and safe streets everywhere.

Formula solution: Experts interested in clean and safe streets everywhere will prepare a self-management plan.

Starting day: 1 May 2021

Ending day: continuous

Salary: From 24,000/year

Possibility of improving the solution or give another idea: Yes.

Comments: People want no unemployment, no homelessness, no begging, no tipping - just all working harmoniously, having good houses, and helping each other. When necessary, corrective medical treatment and significant financial fees will be applied.

Many jobs will be available in this area.

Clean and safe streets + Peace + Freedom + Good Health + Good Family + Good Education + Good Jobs + Harmony = Prosperity + Happiness

France, Paris: The east side of l'Opéra de Paris (or l'Opéra Garnier, 1875), a 1,979-seat opera house, seen from Rue Halévy and Rue Glück.

Formula issue 61. Working for constitution stability

Description: The objective of this issue is to help the Constitution stability.

Formula solution: Experts with knowledge and experience in Constitution stability will prepare a self-management plan.

Starting day: 1 May 2021

Ending day: continuous

Salary: From $48,000/year.

Possibility of improving the solution or give another idea: Yes.

Comments: The Constitution of the World can be improved when 66% of the voters agree.

Great jobs are available for those qualified – it is important to have stability, peace and freedom – then changes will take place in a calm and friendly atmosphere.

Constitution stability + Peace + Freedom + Good Health + Good Family + Good Education + Good Jobs + Harmony = Prosperity + Happiness

UK, London: Looking northwest to the southeast side of the South Building (1899, Astronomy Center) of Royal Observatory Greenwich (1676).

Formula issue 62. Working for space exploration

Description: The objective of this issue is simply to enhance space exploration.

Formula solution: Experts in space exploration will prepare a self-management plan.

Starting day: 1 November 2021

Ending day: continuous

Salary: From $60,000/year

Possibility of improving the solution or give another idea: Yes.

Comments: The purpose for all people on Earth is to be healthy, to live in peace, freedom and harmony, to be prosperous, and to prepare to expand to the Moon, asteroids, Mars, and other places in the Universe, which can support life.

On 18 February 2021, at 3:55 PM Boston time. NASA rover landed on Mars, a great achievement for all people.

Specialists in this area – like rachet production, Earth observation data, orbital operations, ground station networks, launch services, broadband communications, Moon operations, manufacturing in space – will have great jobs.

Space exploration + Peace + Freedom + Good Health + Good Family + Good Education + Good Jobs + Harmony = Prosperity + Happiness

Formula issue 63. Robots and automated processes for people

Description: The objective of this issue is to have many robots and automated processes for people, to live better.

Formula solution: Experts in robots and automated processes will prepare a self-management plan.

Starting day: 1 May 2021

Ending day: continuous

Salary: From $60,000/year.

Possibility of improving the solution or give another idea: Yes.

Comments: It is clear that robots and automated processes for people will help them to live better.

Important immediate objectives for everybody are to reserve time for happiness, use robots and automated processes, work less, and spend more time with your family.

Make civilized behavior and harmony everywhere is an important issue.

Robots help to eliminate stress, and also to help friends and colleagues.

Medical robots can keep everybody relaxed, calm, friendly, patient, and happy.

Experts in this area will have numerous jobs.

Robots and automated processes + Peace + Freedom + Good Health + Good Family + Good Education + Good Jobs + Harmony = Prosperity + Happiness

Formula issue 64. Working to start a new structure of the world

Description: The objective of this issue is to start a new structure of the world.

Formula solution: Experts with knowledge and experience in starting new structures will prepare a self-management plan.

Starting day: 1 May 2021

Ending day: 1 year after starting.

Salary: From $47,000/year.

Possibility of improving the solution or give another idea: Yes.

Comments: To start this new structure of the world, one idea could be this: the first Honorific World Observer (from UN, for example) could invite 10 Presidents form big countries (like USA, China, Russia, UK, India, France, Japan, Germany, Brasil, and Egypt) to be the first 10 Advisors Level 4, starting, for example, on May 1st, 2021, for 10 months, until November 1st, 2021, when the new calm and noiseless elections will take place. The same for the 100 Advisers Level 3, and so on.

It is a little difficult at the beginning, but people will certainly succeed.

Plenty of good jobs in this area.

New world structure + Peace + Freedom + Good Health + Good Family + Good Education + Good Jobs + Harmony = Prosperity + Happiness

Formula issue 65. Helping with books

Description: The objective of this issue is simply to help people with good books

Formula solution: Teachers interested in books related to the new World Constitution will prepare a self-management plan.

Starting day: 1 May 2021

Ending day: continuous

Salary: From $24,000/year

Possibility of improving the solution or give another idea:

Comments: Good books are always useful, especially when people want to achieve peace, freedom, good health, harmony and prosperity.

For better understanding and easier implementation of the World Constitution, the following books, by Michael M. Dediu, are recommended:

- Our Future is Sustainable Peace and Prosperity – Moving from conflicts to harmony and peace
– Our Future Depends on Good World Educations – Moving from frail education to solid education.
– Friendly, Helpful & Smart World Formula solution - Moving from bureaucracy to responsive world Formula solution
– If You Want Peace, Prepare for Peace! – Moving from preparation for war to preparation for peace
– World with One Country & its Ten Friendly Regions - Moving from 195 disagreeing countries, to 1 country with 10 collaborating regions
– After 10,000 Years of Conflicts, People want 10,000 Years of Harmony - Moving from continuous wars to stable peace

- The Constitution of the World – Moving from many unsustainable constitutions, to just one Constitution of the World
- World Constitution Implementation – Moving from violent changes, to smooth transition to the Constitution of the World
- It is getting truer and truer – we urgently need the World Constitution: Moving from anarchic changes, to balanced transition to the Constitution of the World
- World Constitution with Lovely Comments - Moving from many suboptimal constitutions to the much better Constitution of the World
- World Constitution with Questions & Answers – Moving from many obsolete constitutions to the much better Constitution of the World
 - World Projects - Moving from minor projects to great projects for the World
- Dediu Newsletter, Volume 4, Number 12 (48), 6 November 2020 – World Monthly Report
- World Opportunities for All - Moving from few local jobs, to world opportunities for all
- Dediu Newsletter Vol 5, Number 2 (50), 6 January 2021 – World Monthly Report
- Self-Managing World - Moving from local ruling top-down, to self-managing world
- We are all in the same space boat – Peaceful Terra, Moving from local fragile boats to the solid Peaceful Terra
- Dediu Newsletter, Volume 5, Number 3 (51), 6 February 2021 – World Monthly Report

No question that many jobs will be available in this area.

Good books + Peace + Freedom + Good Health + Good Family + Good Education + Good Jobs + Harmony = Prosperity + Happiness

USA, Cambridge, 23 September 2009, on the campus of Harvard University (1636) in Cambridge, The Harry Elkins Widener (1885-1912 (died on Titanic)) Memorial Library (1915, Beaux-Arts architecture, 3.5 M of books).

Formula issue 66. Work for hurricane prevention

Description: The objective of this issue is to prevent hurricanes.

Formula solution: Specialists will prepare a self-management plan.

Starting day: 1 May 2021

Ending day: continuous

Salary: From $44,000/year

Possibility of improving the solution or give another idea: Yes

Comments: Hurricanes can be prevented with some significant engineering techniques – all depends on the good management of this Formula issue.

Qualified people will have great jobs, with beautiful results.

No hurricanes + Peace + Freedom + Good Health + Good Family + Good Education + Good Jobs + Harmony = Prosperity + Happiness

Formula issue 67. Working for long term harmony

Description: The objective of this issue is to create conditions for long term harmony.

Formula solution: Experts interested in working in harmony with others will prepare a self-management plan.

Starting day: 1 May 2021

Ending day: continuous

Salary: From $17,000/year.

Possibility of improving the solution or give another idea: Yes.

Comments: The objective is to have at least 10,000 years of harmonious living on the happy Earth, therefore numerous jobs will be available for everybody.

Harmony + Peace + Freedom + Good Health + Good Family + Good Education + Good Jobs = Prosperity + Happiness

USA, Chicago (1833): above entrance decorations of the Tribune Tower (1925, 36 floors, 141 m, for Chicago Tribune (1847)), with stones from famous places around the world, and from the Moon, including Harvard University, Arc de Triomph, Switzerland, Great Wall, Parthenon, Taj Mahal, Notre-Dame, and St. Peter's Basilica.

Formula issue 68. Working for the new World Constitution

Description: The objective of this issue is simply to promote the new World Constitution.

Formula solution: Experts interested in a much better life using the new World Constitution will prepare a self-management plan.

Starting day: 1 May 2021

Ending day: continuous

Salary: $36,000/year.

Possibility of improving the solution or give another idea: Yes.

Comments: It is nice to know that the Constitution of the World is ready to come into force, and to be put into practice, for the benefit of all people on Earth, on 6 May 2020, and it is ready to remain into force, and enjoyed by all people, at least until 6 May 12020.

Like with any new world structure, it is necessary to explain all the benefits, therefore good jobs are waiting for those interested.

World Constitution + Peace + Freedom + Good Health + Good Family + Good Education + Good Jobs + Harmony = Prosperity + Happiness

Formula issue 69. Working for noise reduction and elimination

Description: The objective of this issue is to reduce and eliminate noise by using advanced technology.

Formula solution: Engineers interested in advanced technology will prepare a self-management plan.

Starting day: 1 May 2021

Ending day: continuous

Salary: $54,000/year

Possibility of improving the solution or give another idea: Yes.

Comments: There are many advanced technologies, which can significantly reduce or eliminate noise everywhere – all depends on the good management of this Formula issue.

Noise has bad medical consequences – it is important for noise producers to have noise cancellation equipment, sound proof walls around them, and noise producers should ask neighbors within 100 m if they are disturbed by noise.

Specialists will have numerous jobs waiting for them.

All people want the Noisy Full-of-Conflicts Planet to be transformed in the Quiet Peaceful Planet.

No noise + Peace + Freedom + Good Health + Good Family + Good Education + Good Jobs + Harmony = Prosperity + Happiness

Formula issue 70. Working for zero-injury everywhere

Description: The objective of this issue is simply to eliminate injuries everywhere.

Formula solution: Doctors interested in eliminating injuries will prepare a self-management plan.

Starting day: 1 May 2021

Ending day: continuous

Salary: From $56,000/year

Possibility of improving the solution or give another idea: Yes.

Comments: Using advanced technology, the injuries can be avoided everywhere.

It is an ambitious project, but good specialists, with many helpers, will certainly achieve the objective.

No injuries + Peace + Freedom + Good Health + Good Family + Good Education + Good Jobs + Harmony = Prosperity + Happiness

Formula issue 71. Working for zero-incident everywhere

Description: The objective of this issue is simply to eliminate incidents everywhere.

Formula solution: Police specialists interested in eliminating incidents everywhere will prepare a self-management plan.

Starting day: 1 May 2021

Ending day: continuous

Salary: From $44,000/year

Possibility of improving the solution or give another idea: Yes.

Comments: Using advanced technology, the incidents can be avoided everywhere.

Again, it is a demanding project, but on a well-managed Earth, it will be successful, creating numerous jobs.

No incidents + Peace + Freedom + Good Health + Good Family + Good Education + Good Jobs + Harmony = Prosperity + Happiness

Formula issue 72. Working for better earthquake forecasting

Description: The objective of this issue is to better forecast earthquakes.

Formula solution: Specialists in earthquakes interested in earthquake forecasting will prepare a self-management plan.

Starting day: 1 May 2021

Ending day: continuous

Salary: $63,000/year

Possibility of improving the solution or give another idea: Yes.

Comments: It is a difficult task, but with more concentrated technological efforts, much better forecasting can be achieved.
Plenty of great jobs for good specialists in this domain.

Better earthquake forecasting + Peace + Freedom + Good Health + Good Family + Good Education + Good Jobs + Harmony = Prosperity + Happiness

Formula issue 73. Other ideas for self-managing opportunities

There are many thousands for very important and urgent world self-managing opportunities, which will employ millions of people for very useful purposes – here are some examples:

- Flood prevention – it is possible with advanced technology.
- Drought prevention - it is possible with advanced technology.
- Dental assistance – all people will have access to good dental assistance
- Trees maintenance – all trees need maintenance, and it will be done the right way
- Sewer maintenance – all people will have public sewer and it will be properly maintained
- Product quality control – all products will be of good quality, for customers' benefit
- Home services – all home services will be easily available
- Business-customer harmony – it will be achieved
- Mortgages for people – less than 5 pages, no fees, less than 3 days
- Global opportunities for all in agriculture, commerce, construction, etc.
- Human error reduction
- Global goal of reducing road traffic casualties
- Increasing personal responsibility
- Aging well assistance
- Cultural improvement
- In the world there are many reasoning errors, false acceptance, knowledge corruption, and obstructed learning, are much effort is necessary to correct the issues.

Jefferson reminds all people: "All tyranny needs to gain a foothold is for people of good conscience to remain silent."

People remember Thucydides: Ignorance is bold and knowledge reserved.

And Leonardo da Vinci: Nothing strengthens authority so much as silence.

Many such self-managing opportunities are waiting to be implemented, for people's benefit, creating numerous great jobs for everybody, thus helping to have a better life on our planet.

Italia, Venezia: the west and south facades of Palazzo Ducale (circa 820 – 1420), and the street Riva degli Schiavoni (right).

Bibliography

- Our Future is Sustainable Peace and Prosperity – Moving from conflicts to harmony and peace
– Our Future Depends on Good World Educations – Moving from frail education to solid education.
– Friendly, Helpful & Smart World Formula solution - Moving from bureaucracy to responsive world Formula solution
– If You Want Peace, Prepare for Peace! – Moving from preparation for war to preparation for peace
– World with One Country & its Ten Friendly Regions - Moving from 195 disagreeing countries, to 1 country with 10 collaborating regions
– After 10,000 Years of Conflicts, People want 10,000 Years of Harmony - Moving from continuous wars to stable peace
- The Constitution of the World – Moving from many unsustainable constitutions, to just one Constitution of the World
- World Constitution Implementation – Moving from violent changes, to smooth transition to the Constitution of the World
- It is getting truer and truer – we urgently need the World Constitution: Moving from anarchic changes, to balanced transition to the Constitution of the World
- World Constitution with Lovely Comments - Moving from many suboptimal constitutions to the much better Constitution of the World
- World Constitution with Questions & Answers – Moving from many obsolete constitutions to the much better Constitution of the World
 - World Projects - Moving from minor projects to great projects for the World
- Dediu Newsletter, Volume 4, Number 12 (48), 6 November 2020 – World Monthly Report
- World Opportunities for All - Moving from few local jobs, to world opportunities for all
- Dediu Newsletter Vol 5, Number 2 (50), 6 January 2021 – World Monthly Report
- Self-Managing World - Moving from local ruling top-down, to self-managing world

- We are all in the same space boat – Peaceful Terra, Moving from local fragile boats to the solid Peaceful Terra
- Dediu Newsletter, Volume 5, Number 3 (51), 6 February 2021 – World Monthly Report

U. S. A., Washington, D.C. (1790) in 2007, National Gallery of Art (1937, in the National Mall).

www.ingramcontent.com/pod-product-compliance
Lightning Source LLC
Chambersburg PA
CBHW041308210326
41599CB00003B/34